BUILDING
EXCELLENCE

BUILDING EXCELLENCE

Implementing Standard Processes For Construction Trade Contractors

MICHAEL KANABY & STEPHANIE SIMMONS

Michael Kanaby & Stephanie Simmons
contact@profitabilityworks.com
www.profitabilityworks.com

Building Excellence, Michael Kanaby & Stephanie Simmons—1st ed.

CERTIFIED

(H)

WRITTEN
BY HUMAN

TESTIMONIALS

When we first started looking at process improvement, we knew we needed to make changes, but we lacked a clear roadmap. That all changed when we worked with Profitability Works. Instead of just giving us recommendations, they used real world scenarios to analyze, implement, and sustain the strategies outlined in Building Excellence. Furthermore, they gave our people the foundations to treat their book of business as their own.

Prior to working with Profitability Works, our processes and procedures varied greatly from location to location. Not surprisingly, our results also varied greatly from location to location. Through their guidance, we learned how to identify inefficiencies, standardize our workflows, and create a culture of continuous improvement. Their detailed training gave our people the tools and confidence to improve our business dramatically.

Since implementing what we learned, we've seen significant improvements in forecasting, change order management, and overall project execution. But the biggest benefit is that we now have the skills to continuously refine and improve our business—without relying on outside help.

That said, knowing that Profitability Works is always available when we hit a roadblock has been a huge advantage. Whenever we get stuck or need guidance on a specific challenge, they're just a call away, ready to help us troubleshoot and keep things moving forward.

Thanks to Profitability Works, we're not just running our business—we know our business inside and out, with expert support whenever we need it. If you're serious about building a more efficient and profitable company, this process works.

Todd Culver
VP Operations
D&H United Fueling Solutions, Inc.

Our relationship with Profitability Works commenced in 2021 and continues to evolve. They have been instrumental in training our project management teams on operational best practices from design to implementation, the same process outlined in Building Excellence. Their construction industry knowledge & advice is deep, practical, and easily actionable. They listen to our challenges, speak our language and tailor practical learning exercises to match our needs—cutting through theory and delivering real-world guidance that our PMs can immediately leverage. The training has significantly accelerated our PM maturity, elevating our team's thinking around project delivery, communication, and accountability.

For construction firms looking to grow profitably and sharpen their operational edge, Profitability Works is a strategic partner worth investing in.

Michael R. Bruno
CHIEF PEOPLE OFFICER
The Arcticom Group

"Building Excellence, as taught by Mike, changed how I lead."

Years ago, Mike trained me on the framework in Building Excellence. When I became CEO of a new company, I followed the same approach on my own. It worked—but it took years. I underestimated how much faster and smoother it would've been with Mike and his team guiding the way. If you know things could run better, don't piece it together alone. Bring in someone who's done it before and can get you there—fast.

– Joe Barber, CEO
Optimum Fire & Security

CONTENTS

INTRODUCTION

Have you been stuck in a cycle where nothing in the business feels predictable, revenue forecasts are unreliable, labor is constantly stretched thin, and just keeping projects on schedule requires endless juggling of crews, equipment, and priorities?

Maybe you are continually shifting resources from job to job, filling gaps yourself, or pulling your top people to cover where others fall short. You can see that operations aren't running efficiently—handoffs break down, communication is inconsistent, and quality slips through the cracks—but you don't have the time or capacity to dig in and fix it.

You are too busy solving problems others should handle—chasing down answers, managing jobsite issues, fielding client concerns, and keeping everything from falling apart. Every attempt to improve systems or drive change runs into resistance—long-time employees push back, your team's "just get it done" mindset clashes with structure, and any momentum fizzles out.

Meanwhile, the pressure on you keeps growing: missing profit targets, risking client relationships, and knowing the business depends on your constant involvement to function. It's exhausting, and it's not sustainable.

If this is you or a manager you know, then this book is the much-needed relief you've been waiting for. It will help the company build the structure, accountability, and systems the company needs to scale, improve margins, and run consistently, even when you are not in the room.

If the business has been built into a successful company through sheer determination of strong leadership but is now struggling with inefficiencies, inconsistent financial performance, or leadership's inability to step away without disruptions, keep reading!

This book is also for those who recognize that while they've succeeded, their company's current methods may not be enough to sustain long-term growth and competitiveness.

If the business continues relying solely on the expertise of individual leaders while maintaining operational inefficiencies, it will face:

- **Limited growth potential** – A business that depends too heavily on a few key individuals cannot scale effectively. When those individuals reach capacity, growth stalls.

- **Operational inefficiencies** – Without standardized processes, projects experience delays, cost overruns and quality issues, which erode profitability.

- **Burnout and turnover** – Key employees and leadership will struggle with exhaustion, leading to higher turnover and difficulty maintaining a motivated workforce.

- **Competitive disadvantages** – Companies that embrace process improvements gain an edge in efficiency, quality, and customer satisfaction, leaving others behind.

- **Financial instability** – Inconsistent revenue and poor forecasting make planning for the future, investing in growth, and weathering economic downturns difficult.

This book was written for construction trade contractors who want to unleash the potential of their business and maximize profitability. This book is not just a theoretical guide; it's a practical tool that can transform your company. You'll learn the steps to take to become a market leader, attract top talent, and revolutionize your business. The best part? These methods can and do deliver quick results when implemented correctly. The strategies outlined in this book are not just theories but practical steps that you can implement to establish the systems, synergies, and processes needed for profitable growth and predictability, regardless of your revenue scale. By the time you finish reading, you'll have the power to make a significant change in your business.

Why should you trust the strategies outlined here? Because we've been at the forefront of numerous transformations in the construction trade contracting industry. We have done things the right way and the wrong way in construction businesses we've led and have seen what works and what doesn't.

We've identified the common thread in both successful and less-than-desirable outcomes.

Profitability Works Inc. is a consulting firm that helps construction trade contractors improve profitability, predictability, and performance by aligning culture, streamlining field execution, and driving continuous improvement. We built the systems in this book to deliver fast, lasting results—and they've done exactly that for our clients. What you're about to read is the same proven approach we use to transform real businesses, every day.

In the following pages, you'll find a clear and actionable roadmap to transition from a people-dependent operation to a process-driven business that thrives on continuous improvement. Each chapter will guide you through the essential steps of process improvement, from identifying inefficiencies to implementing best practices and fostering a culture of continuous improvement. With this book as your guide, you can navigate the often challenging process of change with confidence and support.

Topics include:

- Understanding the limitations of relying solely on people and the power of process
- Recognizing the need for change and overcoming resistance
- Implementing practical strategies to improve efficiency, quality, and consistency

- Building a team and charter for successful process improvement
- Piloting and implementing new processes with minimal disruption
- Creating a culture of continuous improvement and effective change management
- Avoiding common pitfalls and self-sabotaging behaviors

We'll be giving you real-world examples and actionable steps that can be implemented immediately. The book is designed to inspire businesses to transform from one that merely survives to one that truly thrives.

Numerous methodologies, such as Lean, Six Sigma, Total Quality Management (TQM), and Agile, aim to achieve the same results. While formalized process improvement methodologies offer significant benefits, they also present challenges, including resistance to change, high implementation costs, potential for siloed thinking, and difficulty sustaining improvements. We have simplified the process and included steps to eliminate these challenges.

Whether you are a seasoned contractor looking to take your business to the next level, a rising leader seeking to optimize your operations, or a business owner positioning your company for the future, this book will provide you with the tools and insights you need to build a stronger, more resilient, and more profitable company.

If you've reached this point, you are in the right place. No more stagnation, no more relying on unsustainable methods. It's time to build a business that thrives, not just survives. Let's get started and make that transformation a reality.

CHAPTER 1

The Bottleneck Business: When Everything Depends on You

"Trust is the foundation of teamwork. But processes provide the structure that keeps that teamwork functioning effectively."
–Patrick Lencioni

Out of Office

Imagine this scenario: Bill, a seasoned leader of a thriving trade contracting business, had devoted years to building his company from the ground up. After months of relentless work, he finally planned the perfect seven-day vacation with his family, a much-deserved break to recharge and reconnect. As the departure date approached, he felt a mix of excitement and anxiety, the thrill of adventure clashing with the weight of responsibility. The prospect of time away should be liberating, but a nagging worry crept in, whispering doubts into his mind. What if an essential task fell through the cracks? What if an unforeseen emergency arose that only he could handle? Would his team maintain their momentum and meet their targets in his absence?

The night before their departure, Bill tossed and turned, his mind racing with scenarios of what could go wrong. He envisioned a project timeline slipping or a client growing impatient, all because he wasn't there to steer the ship. Still, he resolved to let go of those worries, reminding himself that his family deserved his full attention. After all, he had promised his wife and kids a week of fun, laughter, and a break from the daily grind.

Despite his intentions, as soon as they set off, the familiar pull of his business tugged at him. He found himself glancing at his phone during dinner, sneaking a peek at emails while his children played on the beach. Each notification felt like a small crack in his resolve, and he convinced himself it was just a quick check—nothing more. Yet, each time he responded to a message or took a call, the boundaries he'd hoped to establish began to blur.

The first few days were supposed to be filled with joy: sandcastle building, family hikes, and evenings by the fire. But instead, he felt an invisible tether to his office. Conversations with his wife often turned to work; she could sense his distraction, the way his mind drifted to the office instead of the moment. The nagging anxiety wrapped around him tighter each day, transforming the trip from a peaceful getaway into a constant balancing act between family time and business duties.

When he finally returned home, the weight of the world seemed to settle back onto his shoulders. Instead of feeling recharged, he was met with an avalanche of emails and missed calls. The promised relaxation felt like a distant memory, overshadowed by the same old worries and stresses. He realized that his time off hadn't been the escape he envisioned; instead, it highlighted a glaring issue within his business.

This all-too-common scenario illustrates a problem in many trade contracting businesses: a heavy reliance on individual people rather than established processes. When a business depends too much on key players—like the owner, senior leaders, or other essential team members—tasks and decisions hinge on their availability and effectiveness. Bill's absence not only exposed vulnerabilities in the team's dynamics but also revealed a concerning truth: the business was overly reliant on him.

This dependency created critical issues whenever these key individuals were unavailable due to vacations, illness, or personal matters. Projects stalled, decisions were delayed, and tasks slipped through the cracks. Client relationships suffered as communication faltered. The very essence of productivity and efficiency began to wane, leaving Bill with an urgent realization: if his business were to thrive in the long term, he needed to cultivate a culture of independence where processes and teams could function smoothly without his constant oversight.

The Bottleneck Effect: When Key Leaders Become Choke Points

In trade contracting, success hinges on the efficiency of operations and the smooth execution of projects. This efficiency can become a double-edged sword when a company relies too heavily on one or two key leaders. While these individuals may initially appear to be the linchpins of productivity, their over-centralized roles can create significant bottlenecks, impede growth and negatively impact field productivity.

In many trade contracting businesses, key leaders—such as the CEO or Vice President—are the go-to people for all significant decisions, approvals, and problem-solving. Centralized control can streamline operations in the short term, reducing the number of decision-makers and often leading to quicker resolutions. For example, if a project manager encounters a design issue, they might reach out directly to the CEO for approval on a change order, bypassing the usual channels. While this may resolve the issue swiftly, it places undue pressure on the CEO, who may already be juggling multiple urgent matters.

However, this model is fraught with limitations. When the majority of critical tasks and decisions flow through a small number of leaders, it creates a bottleneck in the system. These individuals can only handle a finite amount of work and make limited decisions at any given time. As their workload increases, the risk of delays and oversights grows. For instance, if the CEO is tasked with approving a budget revision for a major project while also handling client negotiations and staffing issues, there's a high chance that less urgent but equally important tasks—like approving safety protocols—might be delayed.

As essential tasks slip through the cracks, productivity in the field suffers. Crews waiting for approvals on materials or design changes may stand idle, leading to costly delays. Subcontractors might also be left in limbo, unable to proceed without direction. For example, if a project is halted because the CEO is delayed in signing off on necessary permits, it can lead to cascading delays that impact not only the current project but future ones as well.

Moreover, this reliance on key leaders can create a culture of dependency that stifles initiative among team members. Employees may hesitate to make decisions or take proactive steps, waiting instead for direction from the top. This can lead to a lack of innovation and problem-solving at the grassroots level, ultimately limiting the organization's ability to adapt and grow in a competitive market.

In the long run, the consequences of this bottleneck can be profound. Not only can it stymie project timelines and inflate costs, but it can also diminish employee morale as team members feel disempowered and frustrated by their inability to act independently. The organization risks becoming reactive rather than proactive, focusing on putting out fires instead of planning for sustainable growth.

When a Leader Becomes a Bottleneck

Profitability Works collaborated with a company renowned for its expertise in electrical and plumbing installations. Over the years, the company had established a solid reputation, driven largely by a highly respected senior leader who had been with it since its inception. This leader was a visionary, instrumental in shaping the company's success with his deep industry knowledge and keen insights.

However, as the company expanded, it found itself under increasing pressure from a board of directors and investors who had significant growth expectations. This senior leader's deep involvement in every project, while initially a strength, began to morph into a bottleneck that created inefficiencies across the business.

The issue started subtly. The leader was known for his meticulous attention to detail and his insistence on personally reviewing every contract, large purchase, requisition, and subcontractor selection. He believed that his extensive experience gave him unique insights that no one else could match. Consequently, no project could proceed without his final approval. While this worked well when the company was smaller, the exponential growth in workload began to reveal cracks in the system.

The first signs of trouble emerged as project timelines became increasingly delayed. Projects that had once been completed in a week were now stretching into months. Subcontractors waited impatiently for approvals, causing job scheduling to spiral into chaos. Clients started expressing frustration over missed deadlines, and the company's once-stellar reputation began to wane.

Despite these mounting issues, the leader remained steadfast in his belief that his hands-on approach was necessary. He took pride in his meticulous work, convinced that no one else could navigate the complexities of the business as well as he could. This mindset led to long hours; he often stayed late into the night, reviewing documents and making decisions that could have easily been delegated to his capable team.

The consequences of his overreliance began to take a toll not only on the business but also on the leader's personal life. He faced mounting stress, leading to sleepless nights and declining health. His family felt the impact, too, with dinner table conversations often dominated by his work-related anxieties. This stress culminated in a serious health scare, forcing him to reevaluate his approach.

With the business so reliant on him, how could he shift his approach to foster a culture of autonomy and innovation, ensuring that the company could thrive without him at the helm of every decision? By creating structured processes around key activities, this leader could delegate more responsibilities to his leadership team.

The Hamster Wheel of Inefficiency: Stifling Growth and Innovation

Many leaders in the construction industry experience what can be termed the "hamster wheel" effect—a relentless cycle of repeatedly fixing the same problems over and over: delayed materials, missed scope in estimates, insufficient backup for change orders, and the list goes on. This phenomenon often stems from an overreliance on individuals instead of established processes and a commitment to continuous improvement. When firefighting dominates the agenda, there is little room for addressing root causes and fixing the problem once and for all.

Without focusing on continuous improvement, the organization resorts to quick fixes: a band-aid solution here, a last-minute adjustment there. This reactive approach creates a cycle of repetition, where the same mistakes occur repeatedly, trapping everyone in a relentless "hamster wheel."

As issues continue to resurface, the constant pressure to manage immediate crises becomes exhausting. The organization remains in a state of firefighting, which not only hampers productivity but also erodes morale. Employees grow frustrated with the endless cycle of mistakes, leading to disengagement and a reluctance to propose new ideas. When the focus is solely on putting out fires, there is no time or energy left for fostering a culture of learning and improvement.

Moreover, this cycle can damage client relationships. Repeated issues and delays can frustrate clients, leading to a loss of trust and, ultimately, business. Leaders find themselves in a precarious situation: they must react to client complaints while simultaneously addressing the same operational challenges, creating an unsustainable dynamic.

Ultimately, leaders must recognize that by relying too heavily on specific individuals to fix problems, they perpetuate a culture of firefighting, where root causes go unaddressed and mistakes are repeated.

Strategic Transition: Embracing Process-Driven Excellence

To achieve sustainable growth and improve margins, trade contracting businesses must shift from an over-reliance on individual talent to a focus on robust, scalable processes. This transition involves several key steps:

1. **Process Optimization:** Develop and document standardized procedures for routine tasks and critical functions. This includes creating transparent workflows, decision matrices, and approval processes that reduce dependency on specific individuals.

2. **Delegation of Responsibilities:** Empower your team by delegating responsibilities and decision-making authority where appropriate. This alleviates the burden on key leaders and fosters a sense of ownership and accountability among team members.

3. **Training and Development:** Invest in training programs to ensure all employees have the skills and knowledge needed to follow established processes. This helps maintain consistency and quality across operations.

4. **Technology Integration:** Leverage technology to automate routine tasks and support streamlined processes. Implementing project management software,

communication tools, and data analytics platforms can enhance efficiency and provide valuable insights.

5. **Continuous Improvement:** Regularly review and refine processes to ensure they remain effective and aligned with organizational goals. Encourage employee feedback to identify areas for improvement and adapt to changing business needs.

Focusing on these strategic areas can create a more resilient and adaptable organization that is less dependent on individual talent and better positioned for long-term success. Embracing a process-driven approach mitigates the risks associated with over-reliance on key individuals and lays the foundation for enhanced operational efficiency, sustainable growth, and improved financial performance.

CHAPTER 2

Why Change When You've Succeeded with Your Current Methods?

"Survival is optional. No one has to change."
–Dr. W. Edwards Deming

The Comfort of Success

Every seasoned contractor has a story about a project that went off without a hitch—where everything fell into place, the crew executed flawlessly, and the client was thrilled. One contractor recalls a gratifying job where they completed a commercial renovation on time and under budget, relying solely on tried-and-true methods. At that moment, it felt like they had mastered their craft.

However, this comfort can breed complacency. When contractors succeed using familiar techniques, they may become overly reliant on those methods, overlooking the potential for improvement and innovation. They might ask themselves:

"What if my success could be even greater? What if every project could be executed with the same level of excellence?" This reflection is crucial, as it opens the door to exploring better methods and adapting to new trends.

Yet, the construction landscape is changing rapidly, and what worked yesterday might not work tomorrow. As client expectations evolve and new technologies emerge, contractors must recognize that clinging to past methods can hinder their ability to stay competitive and grow the business. By failing to adapt, they risk falling behind as competitors experiment with innovative approaches that can lead to increased efficiency, improved quality, and, ultimately, greater client satisfaction. Therefore, it is vital for contractors to strike a balance between appreciating their current successes and embracing the need for growth and adaptation in a dynamic industry.

Evolving Skills for Future Success

Contractors must reassess their current practices. While these methods may have served them well, they may no longer be enough to meet future challenges. Establishing structured processes can play a crucial role in fostering the necessary skills within the workforce. By creating transparent workflows and standards, contractors provide a framework that encourages continuous learning and skill enhancement. This structured approach allows teams to engage more effectively in training programs and workshops, acquiring new knowledge and best practices.

For example, a regional contractor facing declining margins and increased competition implemented a systematic approach to training and development. By establishing mentorship programs and promoting a culture of shared learning, they not only revitalized their business but also equipped their team with the skills needed to excel in a dynamic environment, positioning themselves as leaders in their market.

Enhanced Customer Satisfaction

At the heart of the industry lies the desire to deliver exceptional quality and service. By improving processes, contractors can ensure more consistent and reliable client results. A streamlined approach reduces errors and rework, allowing them to complete projects on time and within budget.

Imagine a scenario where a contractor implements a new quality control process that catches issues before they escalate. As a result, a project is completed ahead of schedule, impressing the client and enhancing their trust. This kind of experience is what sets them apart in a crowded marketplace.

Moreover, today's clients expect transparency and communication throughout their projects. They want to know what's happening at every stage and appreciate being kept in the loop. By adopting more structured processes, contractors can enhance customer experience and build lasting relationships. Happy clients become repeat clients, and positive word-of-mouth can bring new business.

Creating Opportunities and Engaging Talent

Embracing process improvements benefits clients and creates new opportunities for employees. As contractors grow and adapt, they open up new roles and responsibilities that engage high performers and foster a sense of purpose within their teams.

When contractors involve employees in the change process—through brainstorming sessions, team discussions, or feedback loops—they empower them to take ownership of their work. This not only increases job satisfaction but also boosts retention rates. Skilled professionals are likelier to stay with a company that values their input and invests in their growth.

Consider a construction firm that initiates a mentorship program in which seasoned employees guide newer team members through best practices and quality standards. This initiative improves efficiency and cultivates a culture of collaboration and innovation. Employees feel valued and engaged, leading to higher morale and lower turnover rates.

In a competitive labor market, companies prioritizing adaptability and employee engagement naturally attract top talent. Industry surveys consistently show that skilled professionals are drawn to organizations that are committed to growth and innovation. By fostering a culture of continuous improvement, contractors create an environment that attracts and retains the best in the field.

From Small-Scale Success to Operational Overhaul and Consistent Growth

A trade contractor we worked with had been doing about $20 million in annual revenue for several years with healthy margins due to a loyal client base and strong leadership.

The company's success was rooted in its streamlined hands-on project management approach and close client relationships. The team was dedicated, and the systems they used, while simple, were effective. Though not technologically advanced, their project management process was intuitive and well-understood by everyone involved.

The business had enjoyed steady success and was an attractive purchase. But now, it is a branch of a much larger company, and growth expectations have been high. Fast forward three years, and the company's revenue has skyrocketed to $35 million. The influx of new projects and clients was a positive sign of growth, but it also began to strain the company's existing processes.

The first sign of trouble was a series of missed deadlines. Projects that were once completed seamlessly now faced delays. As the workload increased, the project managers found it increasingly difficult to track progress and allocate resources effectively. The traditional methods that had worked so well before were now stretched thin.

Senior leadership noticed the strain on his team. The once seamless flow of communication began to falter. Miscommunications became more frequent, and tasks that used to be straightforward now involved unnecessary back-and-forth. The team's reliance on manual systems and informal procedures was no longer sustainable. What had been a small, tightly knit operation was now much more extensive with complex needs.

One particularly telling incident occurred on a large commercial project. Due to a lack of updated tracking systems, there were discrepancies in the project schedule. Subcontractors were working with outdated information, leading to conflicting schedules and delays. The project became a headache of missed deadlines, client complaints, and cost overruns.

The methods that had propelled them to success were no longer adequate for the company's scale. They began to see the need for more formal processes and better communication tools.

The company embarked on a transformative journey. It implemented structured project management processes, adopted more formal communication procedures, and invested in staff training. It also improved its resource allocation methods to better align with the demands of larger projects.

The transition was challenging. Long-time employees had to adapt to new working methods, and there was resistance to change. However, as the new processes took hold, the benefits became evident. Projects were completed on time, client satisfaction improved, and the internal team functioned more cohesively.

The company stabilized and positioned itself for future growth in one short year. The new processes allowed them to handle more complex projects more efficiently, and margins improved—a lot. The company now has a reputation as a reliable, high-quality contractor with consistent delivery, making it a preferred choice for general contractors.

While the comfort of past successes can provide a solid foundation, it is crucial for contractors to remain vigilant against complacency. Embracing new processes not only prevents stagnation but also empowers teams to meet evolving client needs and industry demands. As illustrated by the case studies, investing in structured processes leads to improved efficiency, enhanced customer satisfaction, and a more engaged workforce. This transition is not merely about keeping pace with competition; it is about positioning oneself for sustained growth and success. As we move forward, the next chapter will explore why processes are the answer to navigating these changes, exploring how a systematic approach can unlock potential and drive remarkable outcomes.

CHAPTER 3

Why Process Improvement is the Answer

"If you always do what you've always done, you'll always get what you've always got."

–Henry Ford

As the construction industry evolves, specialty trade contractors face increasing pressure to deliver high-quality results in a timely and cost-effective manner. Embracing process improvement is not just a strategy for survival; it is a crucial pathway to achieving sustainable growth and success. Process improvement is the answer for three key reasons: enhanced efficiency and productivity, higher quality and consistency, and cost savings with risk reduction.

Turning Bottlenecks Into Breakthroughs: How Ben Transformed His Business Through Process

Ben owns a company that specializes in life safety installations for commercial buildings. Although his business was doing okay, he began to notice a troubling trend: his projects were frequently delayed, margin performance was inconsistent, and he was losing bids to competitors who promised faster, cheaper results. To stay competitive, Ben knew he had to make a change. So, he began examining his current processes, starting with his project management workflow.

Enhanced Efficiency and Productivity

Process improvement initiatives help streamline operations by identifying and eliminating inefficiencies. For specialty trade contractors, this means refining workflows to minimize waste, reduce delays, and optimize resource allocation.

Consider a contractor who undertakes a comprehensive review of their project management processes. By mapping out each stage of their workflow, they can identify bottlenecks that lead to delays, such as unnecessary approvals or miscommunication between teams. By addressing these issues—perhaps through better scheduling tools or improved communication channels—the contractor can enhance productivity, resulting in faster project completion times.

The benefits extend beyond speed; improved efficiency translates to better resource utilization. With streamlined processes, contractors can allocate labor, materials, and equipment more effectively, ensuring that each project is completed within budget and on schedule. This not only boosts profitability, but also provides a competitive edge in a crowded marketplace and supports growth. Clients are more likely to choose contractors known for their ability to deliver projects efficiently and reliably.

As Ben mapped out his workflow, he identified several key bottlenecks that were slowing his projects down. His team had to wait up to a week for approvals on material purchases, and miscommunication between departments often led to avoidable delays. These small inefficiencies added up, causing projects to exceed timelines and budgets. Ben realized that even minor issues could have a major impact on his bottom line.

Determined to tackle these inefficiencies, Ben introduced a new project management tool that allowed for real-time updates and transparent scheduling, making it easier for teams to track progress and identify issues early. He also streamlined his approval process by implementing a delegation of authority matrix, which empowered team leaders to make quicker decisions.

The results were immediate. With faster approvals and better communication, projects were completed more quickly and with fewer resources. Ben reduced material waste by better tracking orders, and labor costs decreased as teams were more aligned on priorities and schedules. Not only was Ben completing jobs ahead of schedule, but he was also doing it with a higher profit margin. As word spread about his company's ability to deliver quality work on time and under budget, new clients began to seek him out, giving his business a competitive edge and fueling growth.

Higher Quality and Consistency

Quality is paramount in the construction industry, where the consequences of mistakes can be costly and damaging to a contractor's reputation. Implementing process improvements often involves standardizing procedures and adopting best practices, which are crucial steps in ensuring consistent work quality.

When a contractor establishes clear, standardized procedures for tasks—whether it's installation techniques, safety protocols, or quality checks—they create a reliable framework that all team members can follow. This consistency reduces the likelihood of errors and rework, which can drain resources and erode profit margins. For example, a contractor that standardizes their approach to electrical installations not only minimizes mistakes, but also ensures that all projects adhere to industry codes and standards.

By consistently meeting or exceeding client expectations for quality, contractors can enhance their reputation and build trust with clients. In an industry where referrals and repeat business are invaluable, this trust becomes a significant asset. Clients are more inclined to engage with contractors known for their reliability and quality, further solidifying the contractor's position in the market.

Inspired by these improvements, Ben shifted his focus to quality. He knew that one of the biggest issues his team faced was inconsistency in installations. Different team members had different approaches, which sometimes led to errors and costly rework. To fix this, Ben standardized procedures for every type of installation, from designing to safety checks.

He trained his staff to follow these new procedures, which made a big difference. Errors decreased, rework was practically eliminated, and projects were consistently meeting quality standards. Clients noticed the difference, and Ben's reputation grew. Word spread that his company could deliver excellent quality, which helped him secure new contracts and build strong relationships with clients who appreciated his company's reliability.

Cost Savings and Risk Reduction

For specialty trade contractors, cost control is essential in an environment of tight margins. Streamlining processes can lead to significant savings by reducing material waste, cutting labor costs, and avoiding delays. For example, adopting lean construction techniques can help contractors optimize material use, minimize excess orders, and reduce overall project expenses.

In addition, more efficient processes enable contractors to identify and address risks early. Regular reviews and assessments allow potential issues to be caught before they escalate into larger problems. By managing risks proactively, contractors can maintain smoother project workflows and safeguard their financial interests, which in turn strengthens client trust and project stability.

Finally, Ben addressed cost control and risk. He realized that waste—whether in materials or time—was eating away at his profits. By implementing lean principles, he started ordering only the materials his team needed, reducing excess and saving on storage costs. To minimize risks, he introduced regular project reviews to identify issues early. This proactive approach prevented small problems from becoming costly ones, helping him avoid expensive delays and manage his budget more effectively.

These improvements didn't just save Ben money; they made his projects more stable. Clients could count on him to stay on budget, and his proactive risk management approach gave them peace of mind, knowing that he was prioritizing their projects' success and safety.

Through these process improvements, Ben transformed his business. By improving efficiency and productivity, delivering consistent quality, and reducing costs and risks, his company went from struggling to thriving, improving executed margins and obtaining top-line growth. As Ben continued to refine his processes, he found that process improvement wasn't just a one-time fix, but an ongoing strategy for sustainable growth and success.

Process improvement is not just an operational necessity; it's a strategic approach for long-term success. By enhancing efficiency, increasing quality, and reducing costs and risks, contractors can position themselves for sustainable growth and stay competitive. In the following sections, we'll explore actionable strategies for implementing these improvements, helping contractors unlock their full potential.

CHAPTER 4

Productivity Drives Profitability, and Process Drives Productivity

"You cannot mandate productivity, you must provide the tools to let people become their best."

–Steve Jobs

Productivity in construction is a significant determinant of profitability, yet it's often not tracked, and trade contractors sometimes do not understand the drivers. High productivity translates directly to completing projects faster, reducing costs, and increasing profit margins. However, achieving consistent productivity improvements requires more than just urging your team to work harder or faster—it requires refined processes that streamline workflows, reduce waste, and ultimately drive project success.

Understanding Productivity and Its Impact

Productivity in construction is about how efficiently your team can complete tasks and projects. It's not just about speed, but the ability to accomplish more with the resources at hand without compromising quality or safety. Productivity in this sense is measurable:

Productivity=TotalOutput/TotalInput

Total output is the work completed correctly the first time, such as cubic feet of poured concrete, quantity of installed fixtures, or lineal feet of pipe hung. Total input is the total number of hours consumed to perform the output. The output measurement should correspond to the overall progress of the project. If your team can lay a certain amount of pipe per hour or install a specific amount of drywall per day, then any improvement in this rate directly impacts your bottom line.

Minor enhancements in productivity, when implemented strategically, can lead to significant financial gains. For example, optimizing your scheduling so that workers and materials arrive exactly when needed can eliminate downtime, allowing for seamless project progression. Streamlining workflows and reducing bottlenecks—such as waiting for equipment, tools, information or approvals—further enables projects to run smoothly and more profitably.

Consider a scenario where a team experiences an hour of downtime each day due to waiting for equipment. If you eliminate that downtime, you effectively increase the team's productivity by almost 13%, assuming an eight-hour workday. Over the course of a year, this modest improvement can accumulate substantial savings and potentially free up labor for other projects, thus boosting overall revenue.

Bad Process = Waste = Poor Productivity

Inefficiencies, poor communication, and lack of structure in your processes create waste that drains profitability. In construction, waste takes many forms beyond just leftover materials. It can include wasted labor hours, redundant efforts, and unnecessary movement or transport of materials, all of which are symptoms of poor processes.

Common forms of waste in construction include:

- **Waiting Time:** Employees spending time waiting for information, materials, tools, or equipment can create costly delays. For example, if materials are not delivered on time or workers do not have the equipment they need, productivity grinds to a halt. Coordinating with suppliers and managing logistics more effectively can help to prevent these waiting periods.

- **Rework:** Miscommunication and poor planning often lead to rework, which means additional time, materials, and labor to fix mistakes that could have been avoided. Rework is not only a waste of resources but also discourages team morale and delays project timelines.

- **Poor Resource Allocation:** Bouncing field workers around from one project to another without adequate planning often leads to the need for additional labor just to stay on schedule. Overstaffing projects as a quick fix for mismanagement is costly and prevents effective utilization of your workforce.

Implementing well-defined, standardized processes can reduce these forms of waste and lead to measurable gains in productivity. For instance, by adopting a structured handoff process, team members can better coordinate and avoid misunderstandings, which leads to fewer mistakes and less rework. Similarly, improving logistics can help ensure that materials and equipment arrive when and where they're needed, minimizing downtime.

Decreased Customer Satisfaction

Poor productivity doesn't just hurt your bottom line—it affects your customer relationships, too. In an industry where timelines are tight and project outcomes have a significant impact on clients' profitability, delays and poor-quality work can have lasting consequences. When a project fails to meet its schedule or quality expectations, customer satisfaction drops, and so does the likelihood of repeat business or referrals.

A contractor's reputation is largely built on their ability to deliver high-quality work on time and within budget. Projects that drag on, experience multiple change orders, or require substantial rework can harm that reputation and lead to negative reviews, a lack of referrals, and lost future business. In some cases, customers may seek financial compensation or other concessions, further cutting into profitability.

Customers increasingly demand transparency and accountability, so it's vital to proactively manage expectations and communicate project milestones and challenges openly. Clear communication, regular updates, and realistic deadlines go a long way toward ensuring that customers remain satisfied, even if the project encounters obstacles. When productivity is high, and projects run smoothly, customer confidence and trust increase, which can open doors to larger and more profitable projects in the future.

For trade contractors, profitability is intrinsically tied to productivity, and productivity is driven by well-defined processes. Minor enhancements in productivity—from efficient scheduling to clear communication—can have a major impact on the bottom line. Poorly managed processes, however, lead to waste and inefficiency, which cut into productivity and ultimately affect customer satisfaction and the company's reputation.

By understanding how productivity influences profitability, recognizing the cost of waste, and actively working to improve client satisfaction, owners and CEOs can better position their firms for sustainable growth and success. Streamlining processes to enhance productivity is not a one-time task but a continuous effort that requires regular assessment, refinement, and commitment. When done effectively, this approach not only drives profitability but also strengthens your company's reputation, opening doors to new opportunities and long-term success.

A Story of Process Improvement and Increased Profitability

Mike, the owner of a mid-sized plumbing contracting company, had always taken pride in the craftsmanship his crews delivered. But despite strong demand and skilled tradespeople, his profits stagnated. Projects were taking longer than estimated, his crews were frustrated by daily disruptions, and more and more often, customers were unhappy with missed deadlines.

After a challenging conversation with a general contractor who pulled Mike aside about a third schedule delay in two months, Mike realized he had a deeper issue. His people weren't the problem—his processes were.

Mike began by examining daily operations. Foremen consistently reported that their crews were waiting: on materials, tools, or approvals. The delays weren't catastrophic—just 30 minutes per worker per day on average. But Mike ran the numbers: with 12 field employees, that added up to six labor hours lost per day. At an average burdened labor rate of $65/hour, that was nearly **$100,000 in lost productive time annually**.

More importantly, reclaiming that time could dramatically increase output capacity.

Mike worked with his team to overhaul logistics and coordination. Tools and materials were now delivered the day before they were needed. Daily planning huddles ensured everyone understood what was expected. Approvals were pre-coordinated between field and office teams. And they introduced a standardized handoff checklist between scopes to eliminate confusion and reduce rework.

Within two months, the results were noticeable. Crews were finishing daily tasks ahead of schedule. Punch lists got shorter. Rework dropped. Mike was cautious with the math, but even a **10% improvement in field productivity** allowed his team to complete projects faster—without adding labor. That meant his team could take on **an additional project every quarter** with the same workforce.

Financially, that made a real difference. Faster completions reduced overhead per project and increased revenue capacity. By year-end, Mike saw **a 12% increase in net profit**, driven almost entirely by better coordination and process discipline—not harder work.

Customers noticed, too. Projects finished on time—or early. Communication improved. Mike started getting more referrals and was asked to bid on larger, more complex jobs he previously wouldn't have had the bandwidth to handle.

What Mike learned was simple: productivity is the output of process. By improving how work was planned, handed off, and supported in the field, he unlocked capacity he already had—and turned it into profit.

CHAPTER 5

Operational Best Practices for Trade Contractors: Before the Project Starts

"Give me six hours to chop down a tree and I will spend the first four sharpening the axe."

–Abraham Lincoln

Many problems that arise during project execution can be traced back to breakdowns in processes before the work on the jobsite begins. This may include estimation processes and the flow of information from sales, estimation, and design to the personnel responsible for managing and executing the work on-site.

Drawing from years of experience in managing, growing, and working with trade contracting businesses, we've identified key processes that, when disrupted, lead to wasted resources, internal conflicts, and poor customer experiences. Construction companies rely on hundreds of processes, such as accounts receivable, invoicing, and inventory management. However, this book focuses on those processes that have the greatest impact on field worker productivity, company culture, and overall profitability. By mastering these critical areas, you'll position your business for success—not only by boosting financial performance, but also by attracting loyal customers, top talent, and enhancing your company's value.

> Many contractors we work with often claim to have processes for key operational best practices, but these processes are rarely documented, nor do they clearly define what "good" looks like. Instead, they depend heavily on individuals and the knowledge stored in their heads.
>
> For a process to truly qualify as a standard operating procedure (SOP), it must meet specific criteria: it must be thoroughly documented, readily accessible to all relevant personnel at any time, consistently followed, and supported by checklists to ensure uniform execution to the same high standard every time.

Delegation of Authority (DOA) & Pre-Bid Review Processes

Delegation of Authority

Delegation of Authority (DOA) is a formal framework that outlines who must review and approve estimated costs and the written proposal before it is sent to a customer. It specifies the types of projects that require additional review, who the reviewers are, and the expected turnaround time or notice required. Typically, larger projects may involve multiple layers of review based on specific factors, and in larger companies with multiple branches, there might be branch-level approvals as well as reviews at higher levels (e.g., legal, risk, or cash flow analysis).

Failure to have a formalized and documented DOA can cause the following issues in an organization:

- Upper management or board are surprised by a new contract for a large project that is outside the company's risk tolerance
- Repeated mistakes in the proposal writing or terms and conditions agreed to by a salesperson or branch management
- Inconsistent understanding of which reviews are necessary before a proposal is delivered to a customer
- When reviews occur above the branch office, office personnel may not understand why the review is required or may assume that the higher-level reviewer is responsible for uncovering local estimation errors, leading to a lack of accountability within the branch.

It's recommended to analyze historical data to guide decision-making, considering both current and future company priorities. For example, if the company ownership is particularly concerned about risks on large projects, it would be important to create a matrix based on total project cost or customer price. Similarly, if the company has faced challenges with certain types of work or specific customers, those factors should also be considered. Additional levels of review might also be necessary for less experienced branches, salespeople, or contracts that pose higher risks (e.g., liquidated damages, certified payroll).

However, this process can become overly complicated if not carefully managed. That's why it's important to use data to set effective guardrails. Data-driven insights not only help define efficient processes but also provide leadership with the justification for why this system is necessary for sales, estimation, and management teams.

Sample DOA Matrix:

NEW CONSTRUCTION									
SALES PRICE	ESTIMATOR	SALES MANAGER	PROJECT MANAGER	OPERATIONS MANAGER	BRANCH MANAGER	LEGAL	COO	CEO	BOARD
0 - $50,000	1	1	1						
$50,001 - $250,000	1	1	1	1					
$250,001 - $500,000	1	1	1	1	1				
$500,001 - $1,000,000	1	1, 2	1	1, 2	1, 2	1, 2	2		
$1,000,001 - $3,000,000	1	1, 2	1	1, 2	1, 2	1, 2	2	2	
>$3,000,000	1	1, 2	1	1, 2	1, 2	1, 2, 3	2, 3	2, 3	3

RENOVATIONS									
SALES PRICE	ESTIMATOR	SALES MANAGER	PROJECT MANAGER	OPERATIONS MANAGER	BRANCH MANAGER	LEGAL	COO	CEO	BOARD
0 - $50,000	1	1	1	1					
$50,001 - $250,000	1	1	1	1	1	1			
$250,001 - $500,000	1	1	1	1	1	1			
$500,001 - $1,000,000	1	1, 2	1	1, 2	1, 2	1, 2	2		
$1,000,001 - $3,000,000	1	1, 2	1	1, 2	1, 2	1, 2	2	2	
>$3,000,000	1	1, 2	1	1, 2	1, 2	1, 2, 3	2, 3	2, 3	3

In the example on the prior page, the company has separate DOAs for new construction and renovations, as renovation projects typically run into more risks and unforeseen issues than new construction. Depending on what your company does, you may have engineering, design, or some other subject matter expert that you want to include in this matrix as well.

Here are a few important points to keep in mind:

- The "reviewer" refers to a role within the organization, not a specific individual. This distinction is crucial because it prevents the need to update names in standard operating procedures whenever there are personnel changes. It also clarifies roles and responsibilities for employees, helping them better understand their place in the company structure.
- This example matrix outlines up to three distinct pre-bid review meetings, specifying who should attend each level. This ensures that only the necessary participants are included, keeping meetings efficient and avoiding unnecessary attendees. Your company may only need one or two.
- If your company operates multiple branches, some of which are larger than others, certain roles may not exist in smaller branches. For example, an operations manager might handle the duties of a project manager in a smaller office. In such cases, it should be clearly communicated that the operations manager is responsible for both roles.
- This matrix does not define meeting agendas, turnaround times, or notice periods for reviews. Those

details should be included in a separate standard operating procedure that accompanies the matrix.

Pre-Bid Review

A pre-bid review is a meeting held before submitting a proposal or bid to the customer. It includes the key personnel involved in creating the estimate, reviewing the proposal, and those who will be responsible for delivering the project within the estimated costs. This meeting can take place in person, over the phone, or via video conference. The DOA specifies which roles are required to attend and participate in the review process.

Failure to have a formalized and documented Pre-Bid Review can cause the following issues within a company:

- Repeated estimation errors that reduce gross margins from estimated to actual margins
- Failure to clearly identify the scope of work versus excluded work in the proposal, resulting in the company having to perform extra work without compensation
- Failure to identify site conditions that can impact safety on the project
- Failure to identify execution risks and mitigation plans during the estimation process, leading to execution teams scrambling after the job is sold

The purpose of the pre-bid review is not to dive into technical details but to ensure the scope of work aligns with the estimated costs and that there are no errors in the proposal. It's a final check to confirm that the execution teams, who will be accountable for meeting the budget and schedule fully understand the schedule, estimated approach, and customer expectations. This allows them to verify the accuracy of the estimated costs and ensure the proposal clearly defines what is included and excluded. For most projects, this meeting should last no longer than 30-60 minutes.

Sample Agenda

- Customer, location, scope of work
- Inclusions and exclusions
- Approach to execution
- Subcontractor/material bids/pricing
- Material lead times
- Schedule with milestones
- Expected start date
- Manpower needed to meet schedule
- Cash flow analysis (for larger projects that may require the company to finance the first three months of costs)
- Identify medium to high risks to meeting budget, customer expectations, and schedule, along with mitigation strategies for each identified risk

Here are some ways to make this meeting effective:

- Have a formal agenda with roles and responsibilities for each meeting attendee.
- Use standard checklists to make sure key items are reviewed.
- Each reviewer should have a sign-off process retained for future reference.

- Identify who is responsible (by role) to bring key information or validate information before the meeting
- When appropriate, send out estimates, proposal language, copies of customers' terms and conditions, etc., one to two days before the meeting so attendees can be prepared.

The Cost of Assumptions: How a Missed Sign-Off Led to Project Delays and Financial Losses

There was a project to remove old equipment and install new equipment in every classroom of a K-12 school, contracted directly with the public school district. The project didn't have a formal construction schedule, milestones, or liquidated damages for missed deadlines. It was estimated with the assumption that installation would occur during the summer when school was out, and classrooms would be freely accessible. However, this critical detail was never in the documentation given to the project lead, George, nor was he required to sign off confirming his understanding that the work had to be completed over the summer. While one might argue that George should have known, relying on assumptions is a common way to invite failure.

That summer, after the project was sold, the branch took on another large project with liquidated damages and strict deadlines. Faced with a manpower shortage, George, without consulting anyone, made the short-term decision to prioritize the new project and pause work on the school project.

By the time George had the manpower to resume work at the school, classes were back in session. The installers had to work around students and teachers, or after hours, which increased labor costs by 40% compared to the estimate.

Holding George accountable was difficult because there was no documented sign-off indicating that the project needed to be completed over the summer to meet the estimated hours. This lack of communication blindsided the regional manager and caused significant financial issues for the whole region. Had George signed off on this requirement, he likely would have reached out to the regional manager for help with the manpower shortage instead of making the decision in isolation.

An effective Delegation of Authority (DOA) and Pre-Bid Review process offers several key benefits:

- **Aligns with Sales Strategy:** It helps the sales team stay focused on pursuing desirable projects. A more rigorous review process for less favorable work encourages the team to target opportunities that best align with company goals.

- **Prevents Scope Overreach:** It minimizes the risk of unintentionally including tasks in the scope that weren't accounted for in the estimate.

- **Facilitates Early Risk Management:** It promotes early identification of potential risks and allows for proactive risk mitigation planning.

- **Enhances Accountability:** Clearly defined roles and responsibilities ensure each person involved is accountable for their part of the process.

- **Addresses Resource and Scheduling Issues:** It helps identify potential manpower challenges, subcontractor needs, or long lead-time issues early, so they can be addressed before they become critical problems.

- **Streamlines Attendance:** It eliminates unnecessary attendees from meetings by focusing on who is essential, freeing up time for others.

- **Boosts Profitability:** Ultimately, the process helps improve executed project margins by ensuring better planning and decision-making.

Hand-offs

A hand-off is a meeting where a package of information is transferred from one team to the next. It can include job cost estimation, executed contract, ordered materials, work completed, invoicing, and final payment.

Breakdowns in these critical communication touchpoints can result in work being performed outside the original scope. For example, your contract might be based on version four of the drawings, but by the time you're on-site, the general contractor is working from version six. What happens if the foreman isn't aware of which version your contract is based on? They'll likely proceed with the work, assuming it was included, based on what the general contractor tells them. That kind of oversight can get costly!

For every trade contractor, there should be at least two hand-offs:

1. Estimation/Sales to Execution Team (Operations)
2. Execution Team (Operations) to Field Personnel (Site Management)

Additional hand-offs may include design or engineering teams, subcontractors, and a service department once the installation is complete.

At each hand-off, key information must be transmitted and verified to ensure that it's understood correctly by the receiving party. Hand-offs are conducted through real-time, two-way communication — not via email, text, or by simply dropping files in a server folder.

They are important because once a contract or project is awarded, there are often changes of scope between proposal/bid delivery and contract execution (signing). Also, the pre-bid is often months before a contract is awarded, so execution teams need to refresh their memory on key risk mitigation strategies.

It is recommended that the checklist used in the Pre-Bid Review is updated by the person that is reviewing and executing the contract (typically the salesperson or estimator). Then, that same agenda is reviewed in a hand-off meeting with an added section on key contract terms, such as change clauses, the contact person authorized to approve change orders, contract exclusions, and more. The person in the office that is responsible for providing impact notices to your customer needs to understand the time limits in the contract. So does anyone else involved in identifying, documenting, estimating, or getting approvals on change orders in the company (more on this later).

The company may also consider including additional execution personnel, such as a parts procurement specialist, project coordinator, permit runner, or others involved in managing the office work.

Each hand-off in the customer's journey should follow a standardized checklist to ensure all necessary information is passed to the next team. The most critical hand-off after sales to execution teams is from the office to the field personnel. Field teams, such as lead technicians or foremen, need a clear understanding of inclusions and exclusions in the project scope, as they are key individuals that can identify potential change orders. They should also have a general overview of the work required each week to stay on track with the estimated hours. Without clear production goals, field personnel are left to guess whether they're meeting expectations.

Do you provide the total hours to the field team? Some clients express concern that if the total hours are shared, the team will simply use up all the time. While that's possible, our experience shows that employees don't come to work aiming to fail. Most individuals that get clear expectations on how much work should be completed in a specific timeframe will typically strive to meet those goals. They don't need to know there are 1,000 hours estimated, but you should communicate the daily or weekly production targets to keep them focused and on track.

Work Breakdown Structure (WBS)

In construction, a Work Breakdown Structure (WBS) breaks down the project so that those managing field labor can quickly determine how much work needs to be completed per person-hour or day to meet or exceed the project's labor estimate.

The absence of a well-structured WBS and proper training on how to use it is the primary reason project managers fail to identify problems early in a project. The symptom of this issue is that project managers don't realize there is a problem until 80% of the budget is spent, only to realize that they are clearly not 80% complete. At this point, it's too late to recover – there isn't enough time to find out what's causing the issue and to correct it in a way that will impact the financial outcome of the project.

It's common to hear execution teams in meetings say things like, "We have another 1,500 hours, so we're fine." But how do they know? Often, they don't. They may be hopeful or unable to assess how many hours have been used versus what has been accomplished on-site. The human brain struggles to process large amounts of time (hours) effectively to provide daily or weekly production targets for the field.

How does a company set daily or weekly production goals that align with the budgeted hours for the project? It starts with estimation. In 95% of cases, estimators count and quantify materials, then apply a formula to determine how long it should take to complete the work.

> If execution teams are always "giving hours" to the estimators, you are more than likely estimating to your teams' inefficiencies. If a person is responsible for meeting a labor budget and has 100% control over that budget, naturally it will be higher to make sure they cannot fail.

A company needs to establish standard run rates for common tasks and develop a system to transfer these tasks from the estimation phase to the execution team. These run rates can include variables such as working on lifts versus ground level or in occupied facilities versus open new construction. Estimators and field supervisors should have a clear understanding of how the hours are calculated.

For example, run rates could be measured as square feet per hour for surface prep for a painter, devices per hour for an electrical contractor, hours per linear foot for wire or pipe installation, or hours per window or door installed.These measurements will feed into production targets set by the office to ensure the field personnel meet the run rates used in the estimate.

Additionally, there must be a process to receive actual performance data from the field, ideally on a daily basis. This data should be quantified so it can be tracked by the project manager or the person responsible for the financial performance of the project. Relying solely on cost tracking to estimate percentage completion can lead to surprises at the end of a project. More on this will be covered in an upcoming section on daily tickets.

If it becomes apparent within the first two weeks that run rates are not being met, action can be taken to identify and resolve the issue before the project reaches 80% completion, when there may be little opportunity to change its financial outcome.

How a Simple Site Visit Uncovered a Costly Overlap and Saved the Project

We had a client whose current work installed was reviewed against the cost used to date. The cost used to date was 52%, but when the project manager assessed the actual materials installed, it was only 40%. The project manager then went to the job site and found that another contractor (plumber) had installed water lines in the exact location where the sprinkler contractor was approved to install their pipe. When it was brought up to the general contractor, the general contractor made the plumber move to their approved location and the installation run rates improved, saving that job from a very expensive overage in labor.

Adopting operational best practices before a project begins is critical to the success of trade contractors. By establishing clear processes such as Pre-Bid Reviews, structured hand-offs, and an effective Work Breakdown Structure, companies can mitigate risks, improve communication, and align teams around common goals. These practices not only enhance financial performance, but also foster a culture of accountability and proactive problem-solving. When properly implemented, these systems reduce inefficiencies, improve project margins, and position the organization to consistently deliver exceptional results for clients. By prioritizing these foundational steps, trade contractors can lay the groundwork for profitable growth and long-term success.

CHAPTER 6

Operational Best Practices for Trade Contractors: During and Beyond the Project

"Vision without execution is just hallucination."

–Thomas Edison

After projects have been structured to maximize their likelihood of success through the processes discussed in the previous chapter, it is essential for companies to ensure that projects in progress continue to meet customer expectations, adhere to schedule requirements, and remain on or under budget. The following processes are designed to proactively identify potential issues before they affect field execution, uncover additional revenue opportunities, and align the project team with the production rates established during budgeting or estimating. These processes are categorized as follows: labor planning, daily huddles and ticketing, work-in-progress meetings, change order management, and post-project reviews.

Labor Planning

Two-Week Look Ahead

A two-week look-ahead schedule is a tool that outlines where each field worker or crew (by name) will be working over the next two weeks. It is updated weekly by the person responsible for scheduling field workers and should also include the necessary equipment and materials for each job.

If there isn't some sort of two-week look-ahead a company may see that crews are idle on the job waiting for materials or equipment. There may be a project that gets delayed and workers are left waiting to be told what to do because no backup work has been identified for the week. People are bounced from job to job to keep customers happy, sometimes within the same day or week.

This tool helps prevent issues before they disrupt fieldwork. For example, if a job scheduled for the end of next week requires a lift, but the lift hasn't been arranged yet, identifying that now avoids the crew arriving on-site without the needed equipment.

It also improves forecasting accuracy. By planning out what will be completed, revenue projections become more reliable. Additionally, proactive scheduling prevents unnecessary worker movement between jobs or crews being shifted mid-day.

90-Day+ Labor Planning

At the operations or branch manager level, all sold work should be mapped out on a 90-day to one-year projection schedule, depending on the average duration of projects your company performs. Using key milestones from the construction schedule provides a rough estimate of when each project will begin and how many workers will be needed to maintain the schedule.

This process helps identify if the sold (or about-to-be-sold) work necessitates additional field personnel. It will typically take 90 days to get new employees recruited, hired, and onboarded.

This longer-term planning helps identify whether the company is short on labor and needs to hire before falling behind. Involve sales management too, so projected projects can be added to the schedule before contract awards.

This tool can also be utilized to see where the company may not have enough work to keep field teams busy. Identifying this 90+ days in advance allows the company time to make strategic decisions, such as encouraging paid time off, considering lowering margins to get additional work, or refocusing sales teams on the sales opportunities that will fill the gap.

Daily Huddle & Daily Tickets

Daily Huddle

This meeting should be led by the foreman or superintendent and serve as a brief, 15-minute touchpoint before the day's work begins (ideally) or at least weekly if daily meetings aren't feasible. It should start by reviewing the previous day's production against targets. If targets were missed, discuss the reasons why.

Next, address site-specific safety concerns, such as reviewing incidents or identifying new hazards on site. Then, move on to discussing the day's (or week's) production goals. The foreman should actively seek feedback from the crew on any potential obstacles to meeting those targets and highlight what's working well.

This should be a two-way conversation, not a lecture.

If not done or not done well, companies will see a lack of productivity in the field, production rates falling short of estimates, labor budget overages, safety incidents indicating workers aren't following PPE or safety policies, and reduced morale.

Daily Tickets

This process ensures that the actual work completed is communicated back to the person responsible for the job's financial performance, such as the project manager. It can be done through various simple methods—such as a paper ticket, email, or voice memo—whatever is easiest for the foreman to use.

This is crucial because the project manager needs to verify the actual work completed rather than relying solely on costs incurred to estimate the percentage of completion. Additionally, many contractors face strict notice provisions in their contracts for claiming change orders related to delays or changes in site conditions. Missing those deadlines can prevent trade contractors from securing additional time or monetary compensation for the extra work performed.

> **Important Note:** These documents can be discoverable in legal cases, so it's crucial to ensure that foremen refrain from including personal opinions or venting, which could lead to awkward situations.

Daily tickets serve multiple purposes: they track actual production rates to determine early on whether a job is meeting or exceeding the estimated run rates. Additionally, they provide solid documentation for supporting change order requests. It's essential that these tickets are reviewed regularly (ideally daily) to identify potential change orders, flag any project issues early, and ensure the quality of the information provided.

Work In Progress (WIP) Meetings

Work-in-Progress (WIP) meetings are meetings focused on reviewing the status of ongoing projects. These meetings are essential for monitoring project progress, identifying issues early, and ensuring that financial, labor, and scheduling goals are on track.

A lack of effective WIP meetings can lead to financial issues, such as under-billings – when the company is unable to bill for 50% of the work despite having spent 50% of the budget, because the customer can clearly see that less than 50% of the work is complete. Overall, the company may be experiencing negative cash flow from its contracting division. It may also cause additional borrowing for operational needs and an increase in interest expenses.

A standard agenda with defined roles and responsibilities for attendees should be established for WIP meetings. There should also be a documented Standard Operating Procedure (SOP) outlining how to access project financial data, with clear definitions of each key figure. This SOP should be easily accessible to anyone with financial responsibility for a project.

For example, one client's system showed "projected costs" as the sum of actual costs (posted invoices) and open purchase orders, but it didn't account for unordered equipment or unused labor budgets. Such discrepancies highlight the importance of clearly defining financial metrics.

When conducted effectively, WIP meetings enable a company to identify billing issues, improve cash flow, increase change order win rates, and catch problems early—before they affect field workers' ability to complete the work. Over time, attendees will begin to recognize recurring issues that need to be addressed, allowing them to focus on long-term solutions rather than day-to-day project management challenges.

Change Order Management

Change order management refers to the systematic process of handling changes in the scope of work, schedule, or price during a construction project. It involves identifying, documenting, and approving any modifications to the original contract, ensuring that all parties agree on the changes before they are implemented.

Focus on change order management has the quickest impact on gross margins and EBITDA (earnings before interest, taxes, depreciation, and amortization). What we find is that companies that focus on this process start getting paid for work they previously wouldn't have pursued as a change order. Their customers are not creating an unproductive environment anymore, such as re-mobilizations, moving stored equipment, or start delays. They are successful without damaging customer relationships.

Project management teams must fully understand the specific contracts or terms and conditions governing their work, including the foremen responsible for identifying change order opportunities. These opportunities may arise from delays caused by others, changes in site conditions, requests for additional or different work, and similar situations.

All change orders should be tracked in a central system, allowing company-wide reporting. This enables the organization to evaluate how well it is managing and executing change orders. For most trade contractors, change orders should account for an additional 10-15% of revenue.

We've seen companies implement a comprehensive change order process, combined with training for both foremen and operational leaders, resulting in hundreds of thousands of dollars in approved change orders within just six months— without the need for costly software or complex systems.

Notice Provisions: Clauses that dictate how much time you have to provide notice of a condition that is impacting your work. Often, this timeframe is three days, which means if your foreman is made aware of the issue on Friday, you have until Monday (holiday or not) to get that notice to the correct person in the manner specified in the contract. Courts enforce these provisions and contractors know it. Miss your notice provision deadlines, and you're not getting paid – and contractually there is very little you can do about it.[1]

Post-Project Review

A post-project review is a meeting designed to assess completed projects and understand the factors behind both successes and challenges. Many companies only hold these reviews after a

---

[1] This should not be construed as legal advice. See an attorney in your state to review your contract for specifics

problematic project, which can make them less appealing and more prone to becoming blame sessions. To make them more effective and consistent, consider the following:

1) **Conduct reviews for every project:** If that's not feasible, have the sales team select two projects per month and the operations team select two, ensuring one is successful and one is less so.

2) **Use a standard feedback form:** Have each attendee complete a form before the meeting, outlining what went well and what didn't from their perspective. You can also break it down by areas such as design, subcontractor performance, etc. This helps keep emotions out of the discussion.

3) **Follow a standard agenda:** This prevents the meeting from turning into finger-pointing on all sides. Start by discussing what went well, then move on to areas for improvement, focusing on what happened rather than who was responsible.

4) **Create a lessons learned repository:** Record notes from the meeting so that estimators and other team members can review past projects and apply those insights to future jobs for better outcomes. These should be in a searchable depository, which could be as simple as a spreadsheet on a shared drive.

5) **Include all stakeholders:** Invite everyone who was involved in the project, from estimating and contract

negotiation to invoicing and project closeout. Whenever possible, include foremen, as they often provide valuable insights for improvement.

When post-project reviews are conducted effectively, the company can adjust run rates based on improved productivity, learn from mistakes to avoid repeating them, and create more accurate estimates. Additionally, the organization will gain a clearer understanding of the types of projects that are most profitable and can be executed efficiently, allowing the company to consistently exceed customer expectations.

In conclusion, operational excellence is not just about completing projects—it's about doing so with precision, efficiency, and foresight. By implementing and consistently refining practices such as structured hand-offs and proactive labor planning, trade contractors can mitigate risks, enhance communication, and maintain financial control. Tools like the Work Breakdown Structure and structured reviews, from pre-bid to post-project, foster accountability and continuous improvement across teams. These strategies empower companies to deliver projects that meet or exceed customer expectations, while optimizing profitability and field productivity. Ultimately, mastering these operational best practices positions trade contractors for sustained success in a competitive industry.

CHAPTER 7

Self-Assessment Guide: Evaluating the Quality of Your Construction Best Practices

"If you are going to achieve excellence in big things, you develop the habit in little matters. Excellence is not an exception; it is a prevailing attitude."

–Colin Powell

With the processes that most significantly impact trade contractors identified, it becomes essential to evaluate their current state and objectively quantify them across the organization. This begins by determining who should be involved, what questions to ask or observations to make, and recognizing the symptoms of ineffective processes to trace them back to their root causes. The following sections outline the most effective approach for a company to evaluate its current processes.

Understanding the Current State

The first step is for a company to conduct a thorough self-assessment of its current processes. It is important to recognize that the need for this evaluation likely arises from a recurring issue, indicating a larger underlying problem. For example, in construction, a common issue is that projects are sold with an estimated margin, but by the time they are completed, the actual margin is often lower than expected.

Operational leaders, especially those who have been with the company for a long time, may offer quick explanations. They might attribute the problem to errors by estimators, the unique nature of the work, or assume it was a one-time issue that no longer exists. However, a deeper investigation often reveals multiple contributing factors.

Who Should Be Consulted?

Include everyone involved in the process, from the moment an opportunity is identified until the job is fully completed and paid. This includes salespeople, estimators, project coordinators or administrative personnel, superintendents, foremen, project managers, purchasing agents, warehouse managers, finance staff, and others.

It is recommended to engage with multiple individuals in each role or at least one representative from each office or branch. This approach ensures that the observed practices reflect organizational consistency rather than being limited to a single person or location.

Place greater emphasis on the information gathered from those directly involved in the work and on patterns that emerge from independent sources, rather than solely relying on the leader of the department or office experiencing undesirable outcomes. While the department leader may have good intentions, it's natural for them to want to present themselves in a favorable light, which may prevent full transparency.

How Can the Truth Be Uncovered?

It is important to recognize that employees may naturally tell leaders what they believe they want to hear. Instead of asking directly, consider observing situations firsthand. Attending a Work in Progress (WIP) meeting or a pre-bid review can offer clearer insights into what is truly happening.

Tools like anonymous surveys can help gather more candid feedback. Additionally, taking a group of field employees out to lunch—without their managers—can provide opportunities to ask what's working and what isn't. Those directly involved in daily operations often offer the most valuable information and creative ideas.

What to Ask

Avoid closed-ended questions that can be answered with a simple "yes" or "no." In most cases, the answer will be more nuanced or dependent on specific circumstances. Use open-ended questions to gather deeper insights.

Closed-Ended	Open-Ended
Do you hold regular WIP meetings?	Walk me through the attendees of your WIP meetings and outline each person's responsibilities.
Do you do office-to-field hand-offs?	What standard data gets transmitted to field personnel before they start working on a project?
Does Operations sign-off on hours before a price is given to a customer?	What internal process is followed to review a proposal or estimate before it is submitted to the customer?
Do we ever sign a contract for work that was excluded in our proposal?	How often is a contract signed that includes work previously excluded in the proposal?

Open-ended questions provide valuable additional information that can help in identifying the root causes of issues. A good starting point is to ask how each construction best practice is implemented within the company.

Recognizing the Symptoms of Process Breakdown

Nearly any recurring issue in business points to a process breakdown. Senior leaders should be working on strategy, vision, and keeping the organization aligned with long-term goals. If leadership is getting pulled into day-to-day customer, quality, cash flow, or profitability issues, there is a breakdown in processes or a lack of clarity around process ownership.

Efficiency and productivity are the goals at every level within a company. Everyone should have the tools, information, and ability to fully execute their function within the organization.

What Efficiency and Productivity Look Like	Symptoms of Breakdowns
- Actual monthly revenue and margins are within 10% +/- of forecast	- Forecasts are often missed and are a surprise to the person submitting the forecast
- As an aggregate, completed margins are within 3% +/- of original estimated margins	- Large swings +/- on most projects from the original estimated margins to final completion without a root cause identified
- Project execution teams identify when a project is going to exceed budget during the first 30% of the job	- Project execution teams don't identify an issue until 80% of the estimated cost is used

- Design / permit drawings and submittals are nearly always approved the first time	- Design / permit drawings and submittals are frequently rejected or need multiple revisions
- Teams proactively identify problems and take steps to correct root cause	- Teams spend more than 50% of their time reacting to issues

Some additional symptoms of breakdowns include:

- Field workers (including foremen or lead technicians) coming back to the office to pick-up "stuff" during the workday
- Moving field workers between multiple projects during the same day or week (depending on the length of the job)
- Office based leadership/supervision needing to "drop everything" and run out to a site on a weekly basis or more
- Safety incidents that indicate safety policies are not being followed
- Warranty work that indicates lack of quality or attentiveness from installation teams
- Not meeting customer expectations or trouble meeting customer expectations across geographic locations
- Reduced or low close ratios for sales proposals
- Mistakes being repeated
- Frequent lost or missing material

Determining the Root Cause

Many of our clients have shared that they've struggled to resolve recurring problems effectively. This often happens because the root cause isn't identified, and efforts are focused on addressing the symptoms instead. By dedicating time and resources to uncover and address the true cause of the issue, it becomes possible to implement lasting solutions and prevent the problem from happening again.

A very common issue is losing margin from the time a job was estimated and sold to when it is completed. It starts with estimation, contract negotiations and execution, and the flow of information from sales to field personnel, including change order identification and management – and so on. There are so many processes and people that go into executed margins.

Data should be used to gain a clear understanding of what is truly happening. Start by reviewing the last 12 months of completed jobs. Examine the original estimated margins for categories such as labor, materials, subcontractors, and equipment. Identify whether the overruns occurred in materials, labor, subcontractors, or equipment.

Next, analyze the project size, type, and location. Look for commonalities among the jobs where the final margins were lower than the original estimates. Identify recurring patterns or themes.

Are they large jobs?

Are they small jobs?

Are most of them executed out of certain branches?

Do they all tend to be geographically far from a physical office?

Is it with a specific type of work?

Is it the same project manager?

Is it the same foreman?

Are they all with the same customer?

Same designer?

Same estimator?

> **The $300K Oversight: Uncovering the Root Cause of Project Losses**
>
> One of our clients experienced a significant $300,000+ loss in profit on a project. Initially, the project manager attributed the loss to hiring the manufacturer to pre-program the system, which was done incorrectly and required on-site reprogramming. However, that explanation didn't add up. $300,000 for reprogramming? Something didn't seem right.
>
> When we analyzed the data from the job costing system, it revealed that while the programming issue was real, it

accounted for only $15,000. So where did the remaining losses come from?

Digging deeper, we discovered that the client had a subcontractor install the wrong type of wire they had ordered. When it came time to commission the system, it failed because the incorrect wire had been used. As a result, the client had to remove and reinstall the wiring—essentially installing the system twice but only getting paid once.

This case highlights an important lesson: the root cause of a problem is rarely the first explanation given. It often lies deeper, beyond what's immediately visible to those managing the work, and requires thorough investigation to uncover.

Once a section of projects has common themes identified, we can use root-cause analysis to find the issue's primary cause.

Start with a problem statement. What's the problem or outcome that is undesirable? You need to make sure the statement is specific and utilizes data that quantifies the problem.

General	Specific
Customers complaining we are late	50% of the time, the customer tells the technician we are late, however internally we are meeting our schedule dates 90% of the time.

The department isn't meeting budget	Revenue is 20% less than budget, driven by a 40% decrease in the number of large projects year-to-date.

Once there is a clear problem statement, then apply a root-cause analysis.

There are many root-cause analysis methods out there that work. The Five Whys is a simple model that most people can understand and adopt. The Five Whys technique involves asking "why" multiple times whenever a problem arises, with the goal of moving past surface-level symptoms to uncover the underlying root cause.

In his 1988 publication, Taiichi Ohno defined the Five Whys as a simple, iterative technique for identifying the root cause of a problem by repeatedly asking "why" five times. This method, used at Toyota, is designed to move beyond superficial explanations and uncover the fundamental issue behind a defect or problem.[2]

Some problems are more complex, and they may take eight Whys, while others might be simpler, and you can stop at three.

---

[2] Toyota Production System 1st Edition by Taiichi Ohno pg 17

For instance, Taiichi Ohno gives this example about a machine that stopped working (Ohno 1988, p. 17):

Why did the machine stop?
There was an overload and the fuse blew.

Why was there an overload?
The bearing was not sufficiently lubricated.

Why was it not lubricated?
The lubrication pump was not pumping sufficiently.

Why was it not pumping sufficiently?
The shaft of the pump was worn and rattling.

Why was the shaft worn out?
There was no strainer attached, and metal scraps got in.

Consider this real-life construction example: A manager, we'll call him Jerry, was overseeing a large portfolio of about 250 projects, most lasting less than a week, sold by both local and national sales teams. His projects, as a portfolio, consistently lost around 5% in margin (estimated at 35% gross margin, but executed at 30% gross margin), primarily due to labor overruns.

When questioned about the repeated labor overruns, Jerry blamed inaccurate estimates by the local salespeople. However, when asked to back up this claim with data, he found no difference in outcomes between projects sold locally and those sold at the national level.

Next, Jerry was asked to analyze projects where labor exceeded the estimated hours. A pattern emerged: 75% of the projects were day-long or half-day jobs, and 90% of those were assigned to the same technician – let's call him Matt.

Problem Statement: Single-day or shorter jobs executed by Matt exceeded estimated labor hours.

Why One: When asked why Matt consistently failed to complete the work within the estimated time, Jerry explained that Matt couldn't commission or program the systems and required a second technician to finish the job, pushing the project over budget.

Why Two: When asked why Matt couldn't program the systems himself, it came to light that Matt had avoided training for two years by calling in sick when scheduled for training sessions.

Why Three: When asked why Matt was calling in sick, Jerry admitted he hadn't discussed it with Matt.

Why Four: When asked why Jerry hadn't discussed it with Matt, Jerry revealed he didn't know how to handle the situation and had just tried to keep him on two-man jobs. Jerry was shorthanded and needed the manpower. He was afraid of losing the technician.

Why Five: When asked why he was concerned about losing a technician that can't finish a job by himself, Jerry shared that in the past when technicians quit, he wasn't allowed to backfill the position.

The real issue wasn't inaccurate estimates—it was that Jerry hadn't held Matt accountable for completing the required training due to some misconceptions. With his manager's support, Jerry navigated the performance improvement process. Once Matt was placed on a performance improvement plan and completed the necessary training, project margins improved significantly, and Matt was able to keep his job.

Had Jerry's manager accepted the initial explanation, the true root cause, which had affected the business for two years, would have remained undiscovered.

In this example, the root cause and corrective action was relatively simple, but in many processes, there may be five to ten or more contributing factors. Data can help narrow down the possibilities, but some trial and error may be necessary to fully resolve the issue.

Once the root cause is identified and a plan is in place, it needs to be addressed. The following chapters will explore the best ways to build a culture of problem identification and problem-solving by those who are directly involved in the work. This will elevate the company's performance and employee development to a whole new level.

Scan QR Code to Self Assessment Questionnaire:

CHAPTER 8

Building a Process Improvement Team and Charter

"People think focus means saying yes to the thing you've got to focus on. But that's not what it means at all. It means saying no to the hundred other good ideas that there are."

–Steve Jobs

After completing an evaluation of current processes, companies often attempt to tackle all identified issues at once. Yet developing a true understanding of root causes, gathering meaningful input from those closest to the work, and driving widespread adoption of changes simultaneously is rarely achievable.

As a result, when following up three to six months later with clients who halted their efforts at the assessment phase, it is common to find little to no meaningful progress in implementing improvements or achieving better outcomes. In most cases, senior leaders simply lack the capacity to lead these initiatives internally while also managing their daily operational responsibilities.

The following section outlines our approach to achieving real, lasting progress.

Selecting the Right Processes

There are a couple of common approaches to prioritizing which processes a company should address first. The most common and the easiest is looking at each process and mapping them on a continuum, with the vertical axis representing effort of implementation and the horizontal access representing impact on the company.

Each process should be mapped out on the **Continuum of Effort and Impact** below.

In the figure below, each process should be mapped on the Continuum of ease and impact

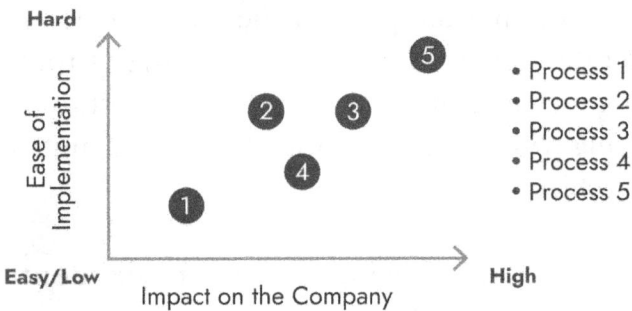

A company can start with ease of implementation for quick wins to keep up momentum, or a company can start with the processes that will have the greatest impact on the company –or a combination of both.

In the Continuum of Ease and Impact chart on the previous page, a company may want to start with Process 1 due to ease of implementation, then Process 3 because it has more impact on the company than 2 or 4, then 2, followed by Process 5, as the team will have better ability to assist with a difficult implementation by then.

Regardless of the approach, it's critical for the organization to ensure it has the capacity to focus. Consider any other initiatives, such as new financial software, payroll systems, etc. Companies that attempt to tackle everything at once often find that nothing gets fully implemented, as there simply isn't enough bandwidth to drive improvement across all areas simultaneously.

Building the Right Team

The unique approach to process improvement starts with a team that will work together to build out the ideal process for the company. There are key positions that are important to the success of process improvement; Executive Sponsor, Workstream Lead, Team Leader, and Team Members. These should include individuals influential with those who will need to adopt the new process. Don't forget adjacent teams or other departments that may be impacted by the process.

How Overlooking Key Teams in Process Design Led to Project Failures

We worked with a client who involved estimators, salespeople, and sales management in developing their pre-bid review process. However, they overlooked a vital group: project managers and field superintendents—the individuals responsible for delivering projects within the estimated costs. When the first project ran into trouble, the project manager predictably pointed to flaws in the estimate as the cause.

The execution team had no input in designing or testing the new process, which was focused on speeding up bid submissions for sales and estimation. This exclusion created a disconnect, leading to increased friction between sales and operations.

We often see clients streamline teams for faster decision-making or limit involvement to those directly affected by a process. Unfortunately, this approach frequently excludes departments that depend on the process outputs, unintentionally creating internal friction. This, in turn, lowers morale, hampers collaboration, and reduces overall productivity.

Role of the Executive Sponsor

The executive sponsor plays a critical role in guiding and championing process improvement initiatives. Their primary responsibility is to identify the key processes that require focus and clearly define the desired outcomes expected from their implementation and adoption. As the organization's advocate for these efforts, the executive sponsor communicates the significance of the team's work, fostering alignment and support across the company. In essence, they serve as a motivational leader, ensuring organizational buy-in and facilitating change adoption.

Regular executive review meetings should be scheduled monthly, providing an opportunity for the Team Leader and Workstream Leader to present progress, highlight accomplishments from the past month, and outline the plan for the next 30 days.

By setting priorities, articulating objectives, and offering timely feedback, the executive sponsor ensures the team remains aligned and empowered to achieve its goals. Their ability to provide direction and make decisive calls is essential to maintaining momentum and driving the initiative to successful completion.

Role of the Workstream Leader

A dedicated Workstream Leader is crucial for ensuring the team's success by driving accountability, tracking progress on action items, and enforcing deadlines. This leader takes ownership of coordinating tasks, facilitating communication, and resolving obstacles that may arise. By maintaining a clear focus on deliverables and timelines, they help the team stay organized, on-task, and keep the forward momentum. Their role is to hold the team leader and the team accountable to their self-identified action items. They may also suggest including different departments, inputting others in the company that can assist the team in resolving an issue. Ultimately, a strong

Workstream Leader keeps momentum going and ensures that initiatives are completed efficiently and on time.

A successful Workstream Leader should possess a variety of key skills to manage and guide the team effectively. Strong organizational skills are essential, as they must juggle multiple tasks, deadlines, and priorities without losing focus. Effective communication is equally critical—both in clearly conveying expectations and in facilitating collaboration among team members. Leadership and decision-making abilities are vital for driving the team forward and resolving conflicts or issues that may arise. This leader must have access and authority in the organization to get additional or different resources to address obstacles the team is facing. The leader should also be adept at problem-solving, able to anticipate and address challenges before they become roadblocks. Finally, a deep understanding of the processes involved and the ability to manage change are crucial, as they will need to guide the team through any adjustments while maintaining engagement and focus.

Team Leader

The team leader should be a person impacted by the process or will need to personally adopt the process themselves. A team leader could be a person that has management responsibility for all the people that will need to adopt the process, however it is not a requirement. Here are some criteria to use in determining a team leader.

- Strong communication skills
- Ability and willingness to assign or delegate tasks

- Willingness to bring in additional team members or additional input as needed
- Have credibility within the workforce that needs to adopt the new process
- Have a clear grasp of why this process needs improvement and can articulate that to others in the organization
- Two to three hours a week to focus on this project
- The ability to stay engaged at work without checking out

Team Members

Team members will be involved in tasks such as documenting current processes, verifying proposed solutions, testing new processes, and getting feedback from others in the organization.

It is critical that the team includes the people that will be using the new process. For example, if a process is to create a new daily ticket, team members should include people that will be using the new daily ticket process, such as foremen, their direct supervisors, and anyone else who will be reading those tickets, such as a project coordinator or operations manager.

When selecting team members, aim for a diverse group. We often advise clients to include representatives from finance, accounting, or other outside departments. An outside perspective can offer fresh ideas or identify potential issues that the core team might overlook.

This team won't just document current processes and define the ideal future state—they'll also be involved in implementation and change management. If a process is going to impact multiple offices, divisions, or brands, ensure each one has a representative on the team. This approach shifts the narrative from "corporate or consultants told us" to "this is a process built by our peers," fostering ownership and credibility within the company. It may even be a good idea to include those that are resistant to change or who may feel like adopting a new process will make them less valuable in the company.

How Involving a Resistant Leader Transformed Labor Management

We had a client—let's call him Alex—who was well-known for resisting changes to his labor management approach. He preferred creating the next day's schedule at the last minute, often texting it to his foreman as late as 8:00 PM, even when the crew needed to be onsite before dawn.

While Alex wasn't assigned to lead the two-week look-ahead labor planning process, he was included as a team member and actively participated in its design and implementation. This involvement allowed the team to address his concerns about the process's value and practicality. As a result, Alex gained a clear understanding of the benefits of planning and how to implement the new approach effectively.

Alex's adoption of the process had an unexpected ripple effect. Others in the organization, knowing his resistance to change, saw his buy-in as a powerful endorsement, which motivated them to embrace the new process as well.

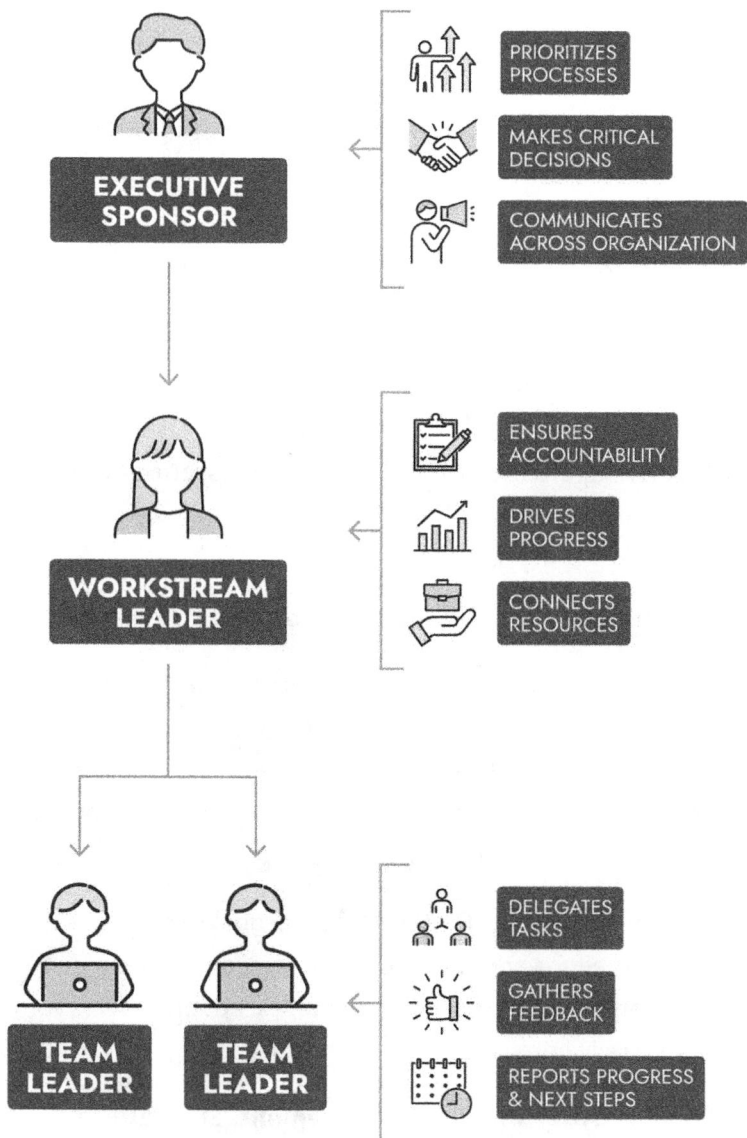

EXECUTIVE SPONSOR
- PRIORITIZES PROCESSES
- MAKES CRITICAL DECISIONS
- COMMUNICATES ACROSS ORGANIZATION

WORKSTREAM LEADER
- ENSURES ACCOUNTABILITY
- DRIVES PROGRESS
- CONNECTS RESOURCES

TEAM LEADER / **TEAM LEADER**
- DELEGATES TASKS
- GATHERS FEEDBACK
- REPORTS PROGRESS & NEXT STEPS

Defining the Charter and Objectives

A charter is a written document that defines the objective of the process improvement initiative and ensures the team stays focused and within scope. It outlines the desired outcomes that will signify successful implementation of the process.

The Objective

The objective is crucial and may take several iterations to refine. The workstream leader should ensure that the objective aligns with the company's goals for the process improvement. Testing the objective against desired outcomes is essential to confirm its effectiveness.

Here are examples of well-crafted objective statements:

Pre-Bid Process Improvement: Enhance and refine best practices in the pre-bid process to increase visibility and accountability for stakeholders, align resources to minimize risk, promote confidence, improve consistency, standardize procedures, and qualify which jobs to pursue.

Go/No-Go Criteria: Develop a go/no-go criteria to ensure that sales efforts are aligned with the company's sales growth and margin strategy. Incorporate an exception process for strategically important opportunities.

Change Order Process Improvement: Standardize the change order process to capture all potential scope changes, improving executed margins. Establish a quick communication pathway for field personnel to relay information back to the office, create a centralized tracking system for change order statuses (pending, approved, rejected), and provide training for field personnel on how to identify change orders.

Key Milestones

Once the objective is defined, the team should establish key milestones. Milestones are the big pieces that will have several steps along the way to complete. These milestones include documenting current processes and identifying existing tools and software in use. It's important to objectively assess all tools and processes, as they may vary across different parts of the company. While people often believe their method is best, a successful outcome usually incorporates a mix of existing practices, unless there is no clear process being followed at all. There should also be a change management milestone where change messaging and communications are built (this is detailed in Chapter 11). It should also have a pilot milestone to try the new process and adjust or fix problems before rolling it out to the whole company.

In and Out of Scope

The next part of the charter considers what is in or out of scope. The Workstream Leader, with the guidance of the Executive Sponsor, should assist the group in identifying what they should be working on and what they shouldn't consider as possible solutions. This keeps the team moving in a clear direction, enabling them to complete the project successfully.

The Pitfall of Undesigned Scope

We had a client who failed to clearly define what was "out of scope" for a team tasked with reviewing how estimates were created. One milestone was to determine if estimators were producing estimates that could be effectively transferred to project teams for setting daily production goals based on the estimators' production rates. However, without clear boundaries, the team veered off course and began exploring new estimating software—something far outside the intended scope. This was problematic, as the company had no plans to invest in new estimation software. Thankfully this was caught before the team wasted too much time.

After the objective is clear, milestones are agreed upon, and in-scope and out-of-scope activities are identified, the charter should be reviewed and approved by both the Workstream Leader and the Executive Sponsor.

Next Steps

Next, the team needs to fill in the next steps, which include activities or steps in the next 30 days to reach a milestone. Each step needs one owner (someone on the team) and a deadline. These next steps should be updated during every check-in with the Workstream Leader and reviewed during executive review touchpoints.

Milestone: Determine all estimating tools used today

Next Step: Corey to meet with Joe to get a copy of his estimate workbook and how he is using it by Thursday next week.

Avoid having one person doing all the work. Steps should be reasonably distributed across multiple people so that no one person has more than four hours per week working on this initiative. Also avoid making the Team Leader responsible for every task. If needed, add additional people to the team if the workload is large.

Key Performance Indicators and Review Results

At a certain stage, the Workstream Leader will need to identify key performance indicators (KPIs) that can measure the current state and track progress as the process is implemented. These KPIs will be essential for validating whether the company is achieving the desired outcomes from the process improvement initiative. This will be highly dependent on available current and historical data.

Some KPIs include:

- Total change order revenue $ / Total project revenue $ = should be 10-15%
- Sold margin $ / Executed margin $ = should be +/- 3%
- Revenue $ vs. Invoiced $ = Invoiced should be higher than revenue in POC accounting revenue recognition

- Minutes to enter a project before vs. after process implementation = should be better after

Successful process improvement requires more than just good intentions—it demands a deliberate, structured approach. By prioritizing processes, assembling the right team, and creating a clear, actionable charter, organizations can focus their efforts on meaningful changes that yield lasting results. Including all key stakeholders, especially those who will directly implement and rely on the new processes, ensures buy-in and minimizes friction. Establishing clear objectives, milestones, and performance indicators further supports accountability and progress tracking. When done thoughtfully, process improvement not only enhances efficiency and productivity, but also fosters collaboration and a culture of continuous improvement across the organization.

SAMPLE CHARTER
Visit the book resources page for a sample charter.
Scan QR code here:

CHAPTER 9

Guide to Piloting and Implementing a New Construction Best Practice Process

"Discovering the unexpected is more important than confirming the known."

–George E.P. Box

A pilot involves implementing a new process within a small part of the business to test its effectiveness. For example, when a company implements a new pre-bid review process, they will typically start using it in one department or location.

When a pilot is launched, it should include change management messaging (more in Chapter 11), training, and process documentation such as a written Standard Operating Procedure (SOP), and, where appropriate, a documented process flow chart or agenda. This will allow the Team Leader, Workstream Leader, and Executive Sponsor to test the effectiveness of the new process, and the associated training and documentation.

The Importance of Piloting a New Process

Piloting a new process before a full-scale implementation is crucial because it allows a company to test, refine, and validate the process in a controlled environment. Here are the key reasons why piloting is important:

1. **Identify Potential Issues:** Pilots help uncover challenges, inefficiencies, or gaps in the process that might not be apparent during planning. Addressing these issues early prevents widespread disruption, which can impact employee morale negatively.

2. **Refine for Effectiveness:** Feedback from the pilot provides insights into what works and what doesn't, enabling changes in the training, documentation, or the process itself.

3. **Build Buy-In:** Successful pilots demonstrate the value of the new process to employees, increasing their confidence and willingness to adopt it.

4. **Train Champions:** A pilot creates a core group of users who are familiar with the process. These early adopters can serve as trainers and advocates during the broader implementation.

5. **Test metrics:** A pilot can test assumptions on a selected metric by identifying how readily the data on the metric is available and comparing the results against the anticipated outcomes to determine its effectiveness.

By piloting, companies can approach change in a thoughtful, strategic manner, ensuring smoother transitions and greater chances of success when scaling up.

How a Simple Pilot Saved a Refrigeration Contractor from Costly Implementation Pitfalls

We worked with a refrigeration trade contractor to develop a streamlined change order management process, emphasizing the importance of foremen and lead technicians promptly communicating changes from job sites to the office execution teams. This was particularly challenging, since most of their work occurred overnight and had to be completed before their customers' facilities opened in the morning. As a result, they frequently missed impact notice provisions in their contracts and failed to secure approval for additional work performed.

We identified a simple solution using their existing software, enabling foremen and lead technicians to quickly document changes via their phones. The updates were automatically uploaded to a database and immediately notified assigned project managers or coordinators.

During the pilot phase, we discovered a logistical challenge: field workers needed their company passwords to add the application to their phones. However, these passwords were typically set up by their managers during onboarding and not shared with the employees. After the pilot training session, it took the office approximately four hours to resolve this issue and get everyone set up—a clear inefficiency.

For the full implementation, we addressed this by instructing local managers to assist employees in resetting their passwords and ensuring they brought the updated credentials to training sessions. This preparation significantly minimized disruption to field operations and management during the rollout.

Had this been rolled out across all 40+ offices without a pilot, the resulting disruption would have severely impacted the overall productivity of the company, leading to a substantial hit to profitability for that month. Piloting ensured a smoother, more effective implementation.

Testing Desired Outcomes

When piloting a new process, it's important to establish a baseline Key Performance Indicator (KPI) and set a conservative improvement target to track success after implementation. As discussed in Chapter 8, these KPIs could focus on financials, time, retention, productivity, or other relevant metrics. The key is that the new process should bring measurable benefits to the company, and the KPI will help assess whether those benefits are being realized.

During the process charter development, the team makes assumptions about the KPI and the expected improvements. The pilot phase provides an excellent opportunity to test those assumptions. For instance, if a company is piloting a new change order management process, one might expect an increase in the number of approved change orders. Metrics such as the close ratio, the percentage of revenue from change orders, or other baseline measurements from the past 12 months can serve as a starting point. For example, if the current close rate for submitted change orders is 22%, the goal could be to increase it to 26%.

Once the pilot is underway, start tracking these metrics as the new process is adopted within the pilot location or department. Setting conservative improvement goals for the KPIs ensures the pilot group has a realistic chance of meeting or exceeding expectations. This not only motivates team members but also encourages positive feedback, which can help ensure a smoother, company-wide rollout later.

Regular Feedback Sessions

Regular feedback sessions play a vital role in identifying necessary changes before full implementation, while also providing an opportunity to gauge adoption and address any remaining concerns or objections from the group.

The Team Leader should hold these sessions with the pilot group or those relying on its outcomes to assess what is working well and what requires improvement. For processes used on a daily basis, weekly or bi-weekly feedback sessions are recommended, with flexibility to adjust the frequency for less frequent processes. These feedback sessions allow participants to suggest corrective actions or adjustments to enhance the process.

Feedback should extend beyond the process itself to include the supporting documentation and training. Were the flowcharts accurate? Was the written SOP clear and comprehensive? Did the training ensure that everyone fully understood their new tasks and responsibilities?

If challenges arise that the team cannot resolve, the Workstream Leader should step in to provide additional resources or support. Any significant roadblocks should be escalated and addressed during the monthly executive progress meetings to ensure timely resolution.

Regular feedback sessions are vital for continuous improvement and successful process implementation. By actively engaging participants in evaluating both the process and supporting materials, the team can make necessary adjustments and address challenges promptly, creating a higher chance of successful implementation across the company.

Full Implementation Strategy

Once the pilot has tested assumptions and made necessary adjustments, it's time to roll out the new process company-wide. There are two primary approaches for this rollout: a phased implementation and a full-scale launch. A phased implementation introduces the new process one department or office at a time, gradually expanding across the organization. A full-scale launch, on the other hand, rolls out the new process to the entire company simultaneously. In some cases, a hybrid approach combining both strategies may be effective. However, regardless of the approach, it should only be considered after a successful pilot phase.

When determining which approach is best, the Team Leader and Executive Sponsor should evaluate several factors: the current level of standardization across departments or offices, the financial cost of delaying implementation, and how significant the change will be for employees at all levels.

Phased Implementation

A phased implementation may be slower, but it can lead to greater initial adoption and smoother integration across the company. By rolling out the process step-by-step, departments or offices can take the time to adapt to the changes without feeling overwhelmed.

Here are some examples of when a phased approach might be more appropriate:

1. **Variability in Tools or Technology:** If different offices or departments use different tools or software that are central to the new process, a phased approach can prevent confusion during training. For example, if the company is rolling out a new estimating process but different offices are using different estimating software, trying to train all offices at once on multiple platforms can lead to confusion. It's best to introduce the new process to one office at a time, ensuring each group gets the proper training for the tools they use.

2. **Other Major Change Initiatives Happening Simultaneously:** If other major changes, like updating payroll or financial systems, are being implemented

within the same timeframe, a phased approach can reduce employee burnout. Employees can only handle so much change at once. By spacing out these changes, the company allows individuals to adapt to one change before introducing another. This can lead to smoother transitions and better adoption rates overall.

3. **Lack of Local Leadership:** If certain departments or offices lack local leaders or change champions who can guide employees through the new process, it may be wise to delay the rollout to those locations until they have the right support in place. Without strong leadership to encourage adoption, answer questions, and provide ongoing support, those departments may resist the change. It's better to wait until the necessary leadership is in place than to rush an implementation that will require rework later.

Full-scale implementation

The full-scale method can be highly effective when there is an urgent need for improvement, and the benefits of the new process can be realized quickly across all departments. It allows for a unified, rapid shift that helps eliminate inconsistencies and ensures that everyone is on the same page from day one. However, to succeed with a full-scale rollout, it's crucial to have the right support structures in place—effective change management, clear communication, and adequate resources to guide the transition.

1. **High Level of Standardization Across the Company:** If the company is already operating with a high degree of consistency in terms of processes, tools, and technology, a full-scale rollout may make more sense. For instance, if all offices or departments are using the same software, systems, or equipment, it will be easier to implement the new process company-wide without the complexities of varying tools or workflows.

2. **Urgency to Realize Benefits Quickly:** When there's a strong financial or operational need to implement the new process as quickly as possible, a full-scale launch allows the company to start seeing benefits across the entire company sooner. For example, if the company is losing money or facing significant inefficiencies due to outdated processes, waiting for a phased rollout could delay the improvement, whereas a full-scale launch may help the company address these issues more rapidly.

3. **Company-wide Alignment and Commitment:** If the company leadership and team members are all on board and committed to the change, a full-scale launch can be effective. This approach works well if there's strong support from top to bottom, with all leaders aligned on the process and ready to push it out to every department. When there's buy-in across the board and employees are motivated for a unified change, the transition can happen faster and more smoothly.

4. **Simplicity and Clarity of the Change:** If the new process is simple, straightforward, and doesn't require

a high level of customization for different departments, a full-scale launch can be successful. For example, if the change involves updating a standardized workflow or a minor update to an existing tool that all employees are already familiar with, there's less risk of confusion or overwhelm during a full-scale rollout.

5. **Strong Change Management Support:** A full-scale launch is more feasible if there is robust change management in place. This includes having clear communication, proper training, and adequate resources to support employees throughout the transition. If the company has a strong internal structure to provide support and guidance during the transition, employees are more likely to adopt the change quickly and effectively across the entire organization.

Whether the team decides on a phased launch, full-scale launch or hybrid launch, the key to a smooth implementation lies in thorough planning and understanding the specific needs of the company. By evaluating the company's current situation, weighing the pros and cons of each approach, and choosing the right strategy, the company can drive meaningful change that benefits the organization.

Piloting a new construction process is an invaluable step in ensuring a smooth and effective full-scale implementation. It provides the opportunity to identify potential issues, refine the process, build internal support, and test key metrics in a controlled environment. By gathering feedback from early adopters, addressing any challenges, and making necessary adjustments, organizations can avoid costly disruptions and improve the chances of long-term success. The insights gained during the pilot phase empower teams to tailor their approach to the unique needs of each department, ultimately driving a more seamless transition to the new process. Whether opting for a phased or full-scale rollout, the lessons learned from the pilot will serve as a foundation for ensuring the new process delivers lasting value and efficiency across the organization. However, the job isn't finished yet. After full adoption of a new process, the teams should be looking for ways to make the processes better or increase its value. This is continuous improvement.

CHAPTER 10

Continuous Improvement: Building a High-Performance Culture

"Without continual growth and progress, such words as improvement, achievement, and success have no meaning."
–Benjamin Franklin

A high-performance culture focused on continuous improvement describes a mindset and organizational culture where individuals at all levels actively seek ways to enhance their work, solve problems proactively, and contribute to the overall growth and adaptability of the business. In the construction industry, where efficiency, cost control, and project timelines are critical, embedding continuous improvement into daily operations ensures a company not only meets but exceeds industry standards.

A high-performance culture rooted in continuous improvement bridges the gap between aspiration and execution, transforming a company's vision into tangible results. By fostering an environment where innovation and efficiency are encouraged, organizations empower their teams to take ownership of their roles, challenge the status quo, and implement better practices. This proactive approach ensures that businesses are not merely surviving the pressures of the construction industry but thriving by consistently enhancing their operations and delivering greater value.

Maintaining a competitive edge requires more than just reacting to daily challenges. It necessitates a culture that continuously strives for improvement, where every team member is engaged in identifying opportunities, solving problems, and refining processes. Continuous improvement is not just a strategy but the cornerstone of a high-performance culture.

Proactive Problem-Solving and Process Enhancement

Continuous improvement is essential for fostering a high-performance culture where teams transcend reactive problem-solving. Instead of waiting for issues to arise, team members proactively identify inefficiencies, suggest innovations, and implement changes that enhance productivity and quality. This shift from a reactive to a proactive mindset ensures that improvements are not sporadic but embedded into daily operations, creating a resilient and adaptive organization.

Key Strategies for Proactive Problem-Solving:

1. **Empowering Employees with Authority and Tools**
   - Provide training on lean principles, Six Sigma methodologies, and process mapping.
   - Establish clear communication channels and structured reporting methods to ensure inefficiencies are documented and addressed promptly.
   - Establish a structured problem-resolution protocol, such as a "Five Why" analysis, to determine root causes and prevent recurring issues.

2. **Creating Feedback Loops for Continuous Refinement**
   - Implement daily or weekly stand-up meetings where crews discuss recent challenges and propose improvements.
   - Utilize digital dashboards to collect and analyze performance data, ensuring that feedback is based on measurable metrics.
   - Encourage frontline workers to submit improvement suggestions, with a formal review process that rewards actionable ideas.

3. **Celebrating Small Wins to Sustain Engagement**
   - Recognize employees who successfully implement efficiency-enhancing changes through incentives or public acknowledgment.
   - Maintain a continuous improvement board in job site trailers or offices, showcasing success stories and tracking progress.
   - Establish an annual "Innovation Award" for employees who contribute the most impactful operational improvements.

Shifting Mindsets and Building Internal Competencies

A shift from passive compliance to active ownership is critical for sustaining continuous improvement. Leadership must model the behaviors they wish to see, fostering an environment where every individual feels responsible for both challenges and opportunities.

Framework for Developing a Culture of Ownership:

1. **Encouraging an Ownership Mentality**
   - Clearly define roles and expectations, emphasizing accountability at all levels.
   - Develop a mentorship program where experienced employees coach newer hires on proactive problem-solving.
   - Hold quarterly "Lessons Learned" workshops where teams review past projects and extract key takeaways for future improvements.
2. **Investing in Skill Development**
   - Offer courses on critical thinking, risk assessment, and decision-making tailored to the construction industry.
   - Implement cross-training initiatives to ensure employees can perform multiple roles, reducing bottlenecks when key personnel are unavailable.
   - Use simulation-based training to expose teams to complex problem-solving scenarios before they arise on actual job sites.

3. **Building Agility and Self-Sufficiency**
   - Develop standardized but adaptable workflows, allowing teams to adjust processes as project demands evolve.
   - Establish an internal "Continuous Improvement Task Force" responsible for monitoring industry trends and integrating best practices.
   - Reduce reliance on external consultants by equipping internal teams with the skills to conduct audits, optimize workflows, and drive change.

Enhancing Processes While Developing People

Adopting a continuous improvement approach not only refines operational processes but also develops the workforce. Employees who actively engage in identifying root causes, collaborating on solutions, and driving change gain valuable skills that benefit both their professional growth and the organization's success.

Tangible Benefits of Process Improvement:

1. **Implementing Root Cause Analysis**
   - Train project managers in root cause analysis methodologies such as Pareto analysis and fishbone diagrams to tackle recurring inefficiencies.
   - Conduct post-mortem project reviews to identify systemic problems and implement corrective actions.

2. **Fostering Collaborative Problem-Solving**
   - Create cross-functional teams composed of project managers, superintendents, and field workers to tackle specific process inefficiencies.
   - Use structured brainstorming techniques like SCAMPER (Substitute, Combine, Adapt, Modify, Put to another use, Eliminate, Reverse) to generate innovative solutions.

3. **Ensuring Sustainable Change**
   - Establish a continuous improvement scorecard to track key performance indicators (KPIs) and measure the impact of implemented changes.
   - Develop a structured change management process, ensuring that new improvements are standardized and consistently applied across projects.

A high-performance culture rooted in continuous improvement is not a one-time initiative but an ongoing commitment. In the competitive environment of trade contracting, companies that embed continuous improvement into their DNA position themselves for long-term success. By shifting from reactive problem-solving to proactive innovation, organizations create a workforce that is engaged, adaptable, and empowered to drive positive change.

The strategies outlined in this chapter—proactive problem-solving, feedback loops, skill development, and process refinement—serve as the foundation for a resilient and forward-thinking organization. When employees take ownership of improvements and leadership fosters an environment of accountability and learning, the result is a company that consistently enhances its operations, delivers greater value, and maintains a competitive edge.

Ultimately, continuous improvement is not just about optimizing processes—it's about developing people, strengthening teams, and cultivating a culture where excellence becomes the standard. By embracing this mindset, construction businesses can not only meet industry challenges but turn them into opportunities for sustained growth and success.

Transforming a Construction Firm Through Continuous Improvement

One of our clients, a multi-branch construction company, faced inefficiencies in managing change orders across various locations. Due to inconsistent documentation and delayed approvals, projects frequently encountered financial losses and scheduling disruptions.

To address this, a Project Manager from a small satellite office was named the Workstream Leader for the change order improvement initiative. Collaborating with Project Managers from other branches, field employees, and superintendents, they:

- Developed a standardized tracking system for change orders and their status and integrating it with the company's work in progress meetings (WIP).
- Created a Project Manager to Field Supervisor handoff package to ensure alignment on scope.

- Established clear guidelines for documentation, approval, and communication regarding change orders.
- Trained staff, including the field workers, on the new procedures and set up a bi-weekly review process to assess effectiveness and make refinements.

Results:

- **Operational Efficiency:** The new process reduced change order approval time from an average of 10 days to 3 days.
- **Financial Impact:** Improved documentation and tracking minimized revenue leakage, recovering an estimated 5% of previously lost project costs.
- **Cultural Transformation:** Employees began proactively identifying inefficiencies beyond change orders, leading to additional process improvements in scheduling and procurement.
- **Scalability:** Other branches adopted the new change order system, reinforcing a company-wide culture of continuous improvement.

Over time, this collective effort transformed the entire company into a high-performance organization driven by continuous improvement. By embedding these principles into your trade contracting business, you'll not only achieve operational excellence but also cultivate a motivated, skilled, and resilient workforce poised to drive long-term success.

CHAPTER 11

Mastering Change Management Through Effective Communication

"We now accept the fact that learning is a lifelong process of keeping abreast of change. And the most pressing task is to teach people how to learn."

–Peter Drucker

Many leaders focus on getting quick results, and that's great! However, many won't achieve process or policy adoption by simply emailing out instructions and telling people to follow them. If leaders become frustrated that their team isn't embracing the "new process," it's likely because they didn't communicate the change effectively. By communicating properly, senior leaders speed up the adoption of new processes across the company. Read on to learn how slowing down a bit will lead to faster, more successful implementation.

From Resistance to Adoption: The Role of Change Management

Change management is a structured approach used to transition individuals, teams, and organizations from a current state to a desired future state. It involves preparing, supporting, and guiding people through change to achieve your organizational goals and outcomes. The focus is on minimizing resistance, ensuring a smooth implementation, and maximizing the benefits of the change by addressing the human side of the transition. This includes creating communication, training, and support strategies to help people understand, accept, and adapt to the change effectively.

For adults to embrace change, they need a clear understanding of why the change is necessary, the benefits it will bring, and the potential consequences of not adapting. Leadership's role is to communicate these points effectively, sparking a desire for change from their direct reports down to the frontline employee. Without this clarity and motivation, adults may struggle to engage with and absorb new information. Training becomes less effective as the learners focus more on questioning the purpose and personal impact of the change rather than the content being delivered. Addressing these concerns in a way that resonates with them is key to ensuring successful adoption.

Once people understand the change, recognize its impact, and are willing to try it, they are ready for effective training to deepen their knowledge. This training should not only target those directly involved in the new tasks but also anyone affected by the change. For instance, if the change involves new software for work order management and scheduling, it's important to train schedulers, technicians, and field supervisors. The company should also ensure that managers and supervisors are trained so they can answer questions and provide ongoing support for those who must use the new system.

As individuals begin practicing new skills or tasks, they won't be proficient right away, so setting appropriate expectations for the learning process is important. However, as they continue trying, their competency will improve. At this stage, it's essential to consider the rewards or consequences (intentional or unintentional) they experience.

Reinforcement is crucial for adults not only to adopt a change but also to maintain the new process or task over time. Both positive and negative consequences should be considered for individuals when they do adopt the change and when they don't.

Before working with us, a client attempted to implement new estimation software intended to greatly reduce the time required to complete estimates.Due to the desire for the change to be adopted quickly, the client hadn't done any change management and started training. They had one office (let's call it Office #1) that had been successfully using the software for years, and they tasked this office with training another office (Office #2) on how to use it. However, six months later, Office #2 wasn't using the software. Initially, it was assumed that the estimators in Office #2 simply didn't want to adopt the new tool.

When looking more closely at what happened, Office #2's workflow required estimators to create estimates and pass them to the sales department. Once a project was sold, the sales department would send the estimate and proposal to a centralized department for entry into their enterprise resource management (ERP) system. Unlike Office #2, Office #1 didn't use the centralized department because they had a separate ERP system.

When we spoke with the estimators in Office #2, we learned that when the sales department submitted the first job estimated with the new software, the centralized department wouldn't accept the estimate in the new format. As a result, the estimators had to duplicate their work by creating estimates in both the old spreadsheet format and the new software. This increased the estimators' workload and caused delays in getting sold projects into the ERP system. Consequently, the new software was abandoned, the change wasn't adopted, and relationships between the two offices deteriorated, bringing collaboration between teams to a halt.

This situation highlights how the absence of proper change management can derail a well-intentioned initiative. If change management had been applied, the managers would have identified the severe negative consequences that adopting the change would impose on the people involved and would have been able to identify how to fix it before they implemented the change.

Communication Strategy: Who

Early communications are to create awareness about the upcoming change and, ideally, generate excitement within the organization. At the very least, communications need to be effective at getting people open to learning more as the change becomes closer.

Start by identifying the people (by role) in the company who will be impacted by the change and how they will be affected. If the change significantly alters how they perform their work, additional focus should be placed on the planning and communication efforts for those groups.

Once you've identified who is impacted, think about how they are affected and consider "What's in it for me?" (WIIFM) for each role. Then, begin crafting your messaging. Highlight the benefits they will receive, the advantages for your customers (since most people care about the customer experience), and the benefits to the company. Examples include making tasks easier, reducing errors, minimizing rework, increasing control, improving visibility, and saving time or money.

At a minimum, your communications should involve impacted employees and their direct managers or supervisors. If the change affects customer experience, include anyone who interacts with customers in the messaging as well. Additionally, you might want to include adjacent departments. For example, if the change involves estimating processes, don't just inform the estimators; include sales and administrative teams who may also be impacted. Their input can help avoid issues before deployment.

Communication Strategy: What to Say

When communicating how the company benefits from the change, avoid focusing on profit or tracking individual performance. Instead, emphasize how the change will help the company or employees better meet customer expectations. For example, if you're implementing a customer relationship management (CRM) system, don't tell salespeople it's just to track their activity. Instead, explain how the data will help ensure operations have the manpower to meet customer deadlines. Just make sure your message is genuine—people can easily spot insincere corporate messaging.

Employees don't really care if the shareholders, owners, or investors are going to make more money. Do not include references to improvements in financial outcomes for the company unless they directly relate to some improvement for customers or employees (such as bonuses or lower selling prices).

Initial communications should be around "change is coming" and it is rarely too soon. It should include:

- What is being changed
- Why the organization is doing it (focused on how it helps employees and customers)
- What roles or employees are going to be impacted by it
- A rough estimate of the timeline

There should then be a cascading flow of messaging from the top down through each layer of the organization.

> **Example:** "Key Construction is working with an internal team of project managers to build a standard change order management process for the whole organization. The goal is to build a process that enables tracking of all submitted, pending, approved, and rejected change orders in each office and on every project. This standardization will help us meet our goal of consistency for regional or national customers between offices. It will also allow our internal teams to better track and close change orders, which directly impact the bonuses project managers receive annually. It will also provide training and tools to foremen to easily submit potential change order situations to the offices for evaluation. We expect that this will start being piloted (location TBD) in August.

When planning communications, consider the medium. If the change affects individuals who aren't usually in the office or don't often read emails, a blast email might not be the best approach. Instead, consider a call or a recorded webinar to ensure they receive and absorb the information. You can also incorporate the message into regularly scheduled team meetings, which might be more effective than a general email.

Communication During the Change Implementation Phase

As the time gets closer to piloting the change with a small group, it's important to ramp up communication with that pilot group. Ensure the impacted employees and their direct managers or supervisors are informed. If the change affects the customer experience, anyone interacting with those customers should be included in the communication. If the change is significant for customers, consider informing them directly as well.

Next, plan a kick-off call or meeting for the pilot group. This meeting should reiterate why the change is happening, what's changing, and the new expectations or tasks for each role. It should also outline the next steps. During the kick-off, it's critical that the team leader emphasizes the benefits of the change.

A kick-off meeting should encourage two-way communication, allowing attendees to ask questions. It's okay to acknowledge some potential drawbacks, such as additional steps, but emphasize that the benefits will outweigh these inconveniences. Along with the meeting, provide backup documentation, including written policies, procedures, FAQs, and any necessary training. Clearly explain the consequences of adopting or not adopting the change. If you've established rewards to encourage adoption, make sure to communicate those as well.

Here is a sample agenda for a pilot kick-off meeting:

- What the change is
- Why the change is necessary
- What roles in the organization will be impacted by the change and how
- Training on new skills (or when training will be provided)
- Expectations on what people need to do differently or next steps
- When and how their feedback will be gathered
- How the impact of the change will be tracked (by data)

Key Roles in Change Adoption

Management of Employees Adopting the Change

If managers aren't fully committed, they may unintentionally—or even deliberately—undermine the change process. Employees typically look to their managers for guidance, so it's crucial that managers not only understand the change but are also motivated to support it. They need to have the resources to answer basic questions and know where to direct issues that arise.

For example, imagine you're a foreman in the field, responsible for getting the job done on time. Your company introduces a new timecard app that every crew member must install, and now you're responsible for reviewing these timecards before payday. This is a major shift for both you and your team, as it directly impacts their paychecks. Now, if you run into a problem in the first week and ask your supervisor for help, only to find out they weren't involved in the training and don't know who to contact, how likely are you to succeed in implementing this change? Not very likely.

Executive or Corporate Sponsor

The executive sponsor serves as the "face" of the change across the organization (or department). They are responsible for communicating what the change is, why it's important, the expected outcomes, and how it fits into the company's long-term strategy. They should also provide regular updates on the progress of the change.

Ideally, this sponsor has direct oversight of most or all the people affected by the change. Employees tend to listen to their immediate boss or their boss's boss, so this role is often filled by someone like the CEO, COO, or a department head.

While the sponsor may not personally craft every message, they need to deliver it in a way that resonates across all levels of the company. Sponsors are typically focused on financial outcomes, but when communicating with employees, it's important to emphasize the benefits to both the staff and the customers, as discussed in the previous section.

Mastering change management isn't just about introducing new processes or tools—it's about navigating the human side of transformation with clarity, patience, and strategic communication. As we've seen, effective communication isn't just a one-time message; it's a continuous, thoughtful dialogue that helps individuals understand why change is necessary, how it impacts them, and what steps they need to take to adapt successfully.

When leaders prioritize clear, well-structured communication and involve the right people at the right time, the transition becomes smoother, more accepted, and more likely to succeed. By taking the time to understand the "why" behind the change, addressing potential challenges upfront, and reinforcing positive behaviors, organizations can foster a culture of adaptability that drives long-term success.

Remember, change is inevitable, but how you manage it determines whether it will drive progress or create frustration. Embrace communication as a tool for growth, and empower your team to thrive in the face of change. The effort you invest in thoughtful planning and communication will not only lead to smoother transitions but also create a more engaged, committed workforce ready to face the future.

CHAPTER 12

Lessons From the Trenches – What NOT to Do

"Leadership is having a compelling vision, a comprehensive plan, relentless implementation, and talented people working together."

–Alan Mullaly

Rolling out new processes should make work smoother, not more frustrating—but too often, companies sabotage their own efforts without realizing it. Whether it's assuming that software will magically fix everything, designing solutions in a vacuum, or failing to involve the right people, these missteps can turn a promising change into a painful mess. In this chapter, we'll explore the most common ways companies trip themselves up when trying to implement new processes. More importantly, we'll look at why these mistakes happen and how to avoid them, so your team doesn't end up stuck in a cycle of confusion, resistance, and wasted effort.

Mistake 1: Poor Change Management

One of the most common and repeatedly made mistakes is neglecting, downscaling, or poorly managing change—often dismissed as "too difficult" or something that "slows things down." The problem is that without effective change management, new processes rarely take full hold. Instead, they end up incomplete, demoralizing the team, reducing productivity, or becoming just another "check-the-box" exercise that fails to deliver real results.

Lack of Change Management Communications

Companies must prepare their people for upcoming changes by ensuring they understand what's coming and why it matters—to them, their customers, and the company as a whole. Without this foundation, employees won't be in the right mindset to absorb training on new ways of working. And if they can't fully take in that information, how likely is it that they'll retain it? Not very. That's when we see repeated rollouts, multiple rounds of training, or, worse, a complete failure to adopt the new process altogether.

Additionally, it's not just those directly affected by the change who need to be informed—key stakeholders must also be included in communications. This includes the direct managers of those adopting the new process, as well as anyone who relies on its outcomes. Keeping these groups in the loop ensures alignment and smoother implementation.

The choice of communication medium matters. Focus on what will best reach and resonate with the intended audience, not just what's most convenient for the company. For significant changes—especially those impacting critical areas like pay processes or essential tools—avoid one-way communication. These messages should always be delivered through a two-way format, ideally by managers or supervisors, to allow for questions, feedback, and real understanding.

Mistake 2: Involving the Wrong People

Failing to Involve the People Who Do the Work

Companies often try to design and implement new processes without involving the very people who will be responsible for carrying them out. This usually isn't intentional – leaders see a problem and try to solve it independently or with others at their level. Once they have a solution, they simply tell the team to start doing things differently.

The result? Immediate pushback.

Employees quickly find reasons why the "new way" won't work or see no real benefit, so they wait it out, assuming it will eventually fade away. However, when the people doing the work are actively involved in creating, testing, and refining a new process, resistance becomes much less likely—because they had a hand in building the solution.

Choosing the Wrong Workstream Leader or Team Leader

We touched on this back in Chapter 8, but it's worth emphasizing—this is critical. If your Workstream Leader is disengaged, cannot get additional resources for teams, lacks a strong grasp of program and change management, or is simply being pressured to deliver quickly, they're likely to make many of the mistakes outlined in this chapter—often without realizing it.

While team leaders are less central to overall success, they still play a key role. If they resist engaging with others, fail to test assumptions, or are unwilling to explore new methods, meaningful progress will be difficult. Another red flag is a team leader who tries to do everything alone. The best processes and implementations don't come from one person working in isolation—they come from collaboration, iteration, and input from those who will ultimately use them.

Mistake 3: Making Assumptions

Lack of Effective Root-Cause Analysis

When we talk to companies struggling with poor business outcomes, we often hear, "We've tried everything," accompanied by frustration over the lack of meaningful improvement. However, when we take a closer look, we frequently find that the root cause was never properly identified. Instead, decisions were based on a single manager's perspective or focused on treating surface-level symptoms rather than addressing the deeper, more complex issue. As we discussed earlier, this tends to happen when senior leaders haven't objectively observed the problem themselves or failed to review relevant data to validate what they were told. As a result, time and effort were spent with little to no real impact.

"Trust, but verify."

–Ronald Regan

Software will Fix It

Software can have a huge positive impact on a business when it's solving an underlying problem. But when software is layered on top of an existing issue, it often makes things worse—and let's face it, most "magic" software comes with a hefty price tag.

> We worked with a client who was planning to invest around $2 million in software to manage project estimates, generate proposals, store documents, track daily work tickets, schedule, and plan labor. Their goal was to improve project margins by reducing estimation errors. However, after suggesting they evaluate their current estimation tools and processes, we discovered that the majority of errors came from estimators not physically seeing the work they were estimating for repairs. While the software could help in certain areas, it wouldn't fix the core human issue causing most of the errors.

Software can certainly be part of a solution, but it's rarely the silver bullet solution—unless we're talking about ERPs or financial tracking systems. It's crucial to ensure your team can identify the real causes of today's issues and determine how software can effectively address those core problems.

Mistake 4: Lack of Proper Documentation

For a new process to truly become ingrained in a company's culture, it needs to be standardized, documented, and accessible to everyone who manages, contributes to, or depends on the process. This means making sure the process is available to those responsible for executing it, as well as those who need to review or rely on its outcomes.

Sending an Email is Risky

How many emails do your employees get each day? Chances are, if a new process is shared via email, it will quickly get buried and forgotten. That email won't help anyone when they need to onboard a new team member, prepare for a performance review, or reference the process down the line. Instead, the process needs to be stored in a central location—such as a shared drive—that's accessible to the right people, ideally on mobile devices.

Incorrect or Missing Roles and Responsibilities

A common mistake in process design is failing to clearly define roles and responsibilities. Without clearly stating who is responsible for each step, confusion and inefficiencies will inevitably arise. This leads to delays, duplicated efforts, and unmet goals. By establishing clear roles and responsibilities from the beginning, management can streamline operations, hold individuals accountable, and ensure the project progresses smoothly toward successful completion.

One major pitfall is assigning individual names to each step of a process, rather than defining roles within the organization. This often happens because job titles don't always align with actual responsibilities. For example, someone who primarily handles labor scheduling may be labeled as a project manager, construction manager, or superintendent, depending on the office.

When processes rely on individual names, issues arise when people leave. If Bill is responsible for a specific task and then departs, it can trigger a blame game: "That was Bill's job." When responsibility shifts to a new person, the step in the SOP should shift with it, ensuring continuity. By focusing on roles rather than individual names, the process becomes more adaptable, allowing for smoother transitions when team changes occur.

To avoid this, it's better to define responsibilities instead of titles. For example, an SOP for two-week look-ahead planning could specify that the person responsible for scheduling foremen and crews is tasked with updating the look-ahead every Friday by 10am. This could be an operations manager in one office, a project coordinator in another, or a superintendent elsewhere. This ensures that the company has one consistent SOP across all offices, regardless of different roles in different locations.

Additionally, if the primary person responsible for a task is out on vacation or leaves the company, the SOP should make it clear that the responsibility shifts to the individual that is taking on the responsibility to schedule foremen and crews. This ensures that the process continues seamlessly, whether the transition is temporary or permanent.

Defining What "Good" Looks Like for Key Steps

Many processes require individuals to input information, but without clear guidance, the level of detail can vary based on personal work styles. Some people are naturally more detail-oriented than others. To ensure consistency, it's essential to define what information should be included and establish a timeline for each step.

> For example, one client attempted to improve estimate accuracy by having salespeople submit key project details through Microsoft Forms linked to their phones. This was a smart, low-cost solution that clearly outlined the required information for estimators.
>
> However, the company made a critical oversight: they didn't define the expected quality of responses. While each field was required, salespeople quickly realized they could bypass questions by entering "N/A." Without clear guidelines on acceptable responses, the form was completed, but the goal of improving estimate accuracy was not achieved.

This highlights a common challenge in process improvement— assuming that a tool alone will solve the problem. Successful implementation requires more than just a new system; it demands clear communication, well-defined expectations, and engagement from those responsible for execution. By setting clear standards for each step, organizations can avoid pitfalls and ensure meaningful improvements.

Implementing new processes can be a transformative opportunity for a company, but it is all too easy to make mistakes that undermine the intended results. From neglecting change management to assuming that software alone will fix problems, these missteps can derail progress and frustrate employees. Clear communication, thoughtful planning, and thorough involvement of those doing the work are essential for success. By avoiding the common pitfalls outlined in this chapter and focusing on defining roles, responsibilities, and expectations from the outset, organizations can ensure smoother transitions and more meaningful improvements. Effective change requires more than just a plan—it requires commitment, attention to detail, and a willingness to adapt based on real insights and feedback.

CONCLUSION

From Blueprint to Breakthrough

Congratulations on reaching the end! You now understand the power of reducing reliance on individuals and focusing on mastering processes to eliminate inefficiencies. You've seen how communication and change management drive maximum adoption and create a high-performance culture. However, knowledge without action is like having a blueprint without building anything.

This book isn't just theory—it's a call to action. The construction industry thrives on execution, and your business is no different. You've learned how relying on individuals leads to inconsistency, limits growth, and prevents true freedom. However, implementing critical processes isn't just about efficiency; it's about creating a sustainable, scalable, and more profitable business. The difference between surviving and thriving lies in your willingness to step outside your comfort zone, embrace change, and implement the strategies outlined in these pages. Procrastination and outdated methods will only perpetuate the challenges you seek to overcome.

The sooner your company implements standardized processes, the quicker the problems will diminish—often within six to twelve months. And the issues you see today are just the surface. Hidden inefficiencies—like the client whose project booking process wasted 27 minutes per entry—are draining your resources in ways you may not even realize. Simple improvements, such as standardizing workflows, can reclaim valuable time and dramatically improve efficiency, allowing your team to focus on higher-value tasks.

The Future You Can Build

Imagine a future where your projects run smoothly, consistently delivering high-quality results. Picture an empowered, proactive team that works efficiently instead of reactively. Envision a business that attracts and retains top talent, is known for reliability and excellence, and consistently exceeds profit expectations. A well-structured company, where frontline and middle managers actively identify root causes, refine processes, and create lasting improvements, will drive greater financial predictability and eliminate costly fluctuations between financial periods. This is what's possible through process improvement.

The High Cost of Inaction

Maintaining the status quo may feel easier in the short term, but the risks of stagnation compound over time, threatening the very survival of your business. Competitors who embrace process improvement gain a distinct advantage, refining their operations, reducing inefficiencies, and delivering superior results. Without structured improvements, your growth becomes stunted. Instead of focusing on innovation and expansion, you'll be stuck putting out fires, limiting your ability to scale effectively.

Profitability will suffer as inefficiencies, errors, and project delays erode margins. What may seem like minor inefficiencies accumulate over time, significantly impacting your bottom line. Beyond financial losses, a lack of clear processes leads to employee burnout, high turnover, and operational instability. Without structured systems, teams rely on guesswork and individual effort, resulting in stress and frustration.

Your reputation is also at stake. Inconsistent quality, missed deadlines, and poor project management damage client trust, leading to fewer referrals and lost business opportunities. In an industry where reputation is everything, failure to meet expectations can have long-term consequences.

Ultimately, refusing to evolve puts your company at risk of being left behind in a field defined by tight margins, fierce competition, and a constant battle for top talent. The choice is clear—invest in process improvement or face the mounting costs of inaction later.

Your Next Steps

You now have the tools, the roadmap, and the knowledge to create meaningful change in your business. This book has given you the framework to implement process improvements, reduce inefficiencies, and build a stronger, more scalable company. You can absolutely take what you've learned and apply it yourself—many successful businesses have done just that.

However, knowledge alone doesn't guarantee execution. Even the best strategies can fall short without the right support, guidance, and accountability. Working with a professional doesn't replace what you've learned—it accelerates its impact. An expert can help you identify blind spots, tailor solutions to your specific challenges, and ensure smooth implementation, reducing trial and error. What might take months—or even years—to refine on your own can be streamlined into a structured, results-driven process that delivers measurable improvements faster.

The real question isn't whether you can do this alone—it's how much further ahead you could be with the right expertise guiding you. Now is the time to act.

If you're ready to implement these strategies faster and with greater impact, let's talk. Reach out today to discuss how expert guidance can help you achieve measurable results—quickly and efficiently. The sooner you start, the sooner you'll see the benefits.

Your business's future is in your hands. Build it.

Take the Next Step Toward Profitable Growth

If this book sparked ideas or confirmed challenges you're ready to tackle, we invite you to stay connected and explore how we can help:

1. Follow *Profitability Works* on LinkedIn for weekly insights, tips, and stories from the field. Scan QR Code:

2. Subscribe to our newsletter for practical tools and strategies to improve processes and profitability in your construction business. Scan QR Code

3. Schedule a conversation with us to see if we're the right fit to support your implementation journey. Scan QR Code:

Visit **www.profitabilityworks.com** to get started.

ABOUT THE AUTHOR

Michael Kanaby, Managing Partner of Profitability Works Inc., has over 30 years of experience in construction, from field positions to executive leadership in publicly traded construction organizations. His focus areas include productivity and process improvements, strategy, leadership development, and project management excellence. Michael holds a BA in Organizational Development, Masters of Business Administration (MBA), is a Certified Lean Six Sigma Black Belt (CLSBB), a Project Management Professional (PMP), Project Management Institute Construction professional (PMI-CP), holds a Graduate Certificate in Project Management, and is a graduate of the Executive Education Program at the Wharton School of Business. Michael is also a proud US Army Veteran.

Stephanie Simmons leads and supports client engagements around change management, sales growth, organizational communication, transformation, and leadership development. Prior to founding Profitability Works Inc., Stephanie worked within a large global publicly traded construction company and led organizational transformations, integrating new mergers/acquisitions change initiatives while also leading a large part of the sales organization in North America. Stephanie served 24 years in various roles within trade contractors in sales, general management, and leading organizational transformations. This experience has offered her unique capabilities to assist teams in implementing change to improve profitability. Stephanie holds a Bachelor of Science in Business Administration, is a Certified Coach, and is trained in ADKAR ® Change Management methods.

www.ingramcontent.com/pod-product-compliance
Lightning Source LLC
Chambersburg PA
CBHW071556200326
41519CB00021BB/6771